Layman's Bible Book Commentary
Exodus

LAYMAN'S BIBLE BOOK COMMENTARY

LBBC

EXODUS

VOLUME 2

Robert L. Cate

BROADMAN PRESS
Nashville, Tennessee

Dedicated to Dot
My companion in our journey with God

4211–72
ISBN: 0–8054–1172–0

Dewey Decimal Classification: 222.12
Subject heading: BIBLE. O. T. EXODUS

Library of Congress Catalog Card Number: 78–059976
Printed in the United States of America

Foreword

The *Layman's Bible Book Commentary* in twenty-four volumes was planned as a practical exposition of the whole Bible for lay readers and students. It is based on the conviction that the Bible speaks to every generation of believers but needs occasional reinterpretation in the light of changing language and modern experience. Following the guidance of God's Spirit, the believer finds in it the authoritative word for faith and life.

To meet the needs of lay readers, the *Commentary* is written in a popular style, and each Bible book is clearly outlined to reveal its major emphases. Although the writers are competent scholars and reverent interpreters, they have avoided critical problems and the use of original languages except where they were essential for explaining the text. They recognize the variety of literary forms in the Bible, but they have not followed documentary trails or become preoccupied with literary concerns. Their primary purpose was to show what each Bible book meant for its time and what it says to our own generation.

The Revised Standard Version of the Bible is the basic text of the *Commentary,* but writers were free to use other translations to clarify an occasional passage or sharpen its effect. To provide as much interpretation as possible in such concise books, the Bible text was not printed along with the comment.

Of the twenty-four volumes of the *Commentary,* fourteen deal with Old Testament books and ten with those in the New Testament. The volumes range in pages from 140 to 168. Four major books in the Old Testament and five in the New are treated in one volume each. Others appear in various combinations. Although the allotted space varies, each Bible book is treated as a whole to reveal its basic message with some passages getting special attention. Whatever plan of Bible study the reader may follow, this *Commentary* will be a valuable companion.

Despite the best-seller reputation of the Bible, the average survey of Bible knowledge reveals a good deal of ignorance about it and its primary meaning. Many adult church members seem to think that its study is intended for children and preachers. But some of the newer translations have been making the Bible more readable for all ages. Bible study has branched out from Sunday into other days of the week, and into neighborhoods rather than just in churches. This *Commentary* wants to meet the growing need for insight into all that the Bible has to say about God and his world and about Christ and his fellowship.

BROADMAN PRESS

Contents

Introduction:
The Book of Exodus

The book of Exodus is one of the most important books in the Old Testament, and it is also fascinating. Its fascination lies in the readable and dramatic account of Israel's exodus from Egypt under the human leadership of Moses and the divine leadership of the God of Abraham. In this exodus Israel made a geographical pilgrimage from Egypt to Sinai, a social pilgrimage from slavery to freedom, and a spiritual pilgrimage from being merely the sons of Israel to being the covenant people of God.

In these pages the towering figure of Moses dominates the entire scene. But even though his presence pervades and overshadows every episode, two things become very obvious. He is always presented as receiving his authority and power from God. Further, he is never presented as anything more than a man with all of the weakness which that implies.

The importance of Exodus, however, lies in far more than its dramatic impact. It is not merely a human story; it is a divine story as well. It records a part of God's redemptive activity in history. Exodus tells how God prepared a man, beginning his preparation long before the man even knew it. It exposes for our study the ways in which God dealt with both the sin and stubbornness of Moses, transforming him into the greatest man of faith and prayer in the Old Testament. Then it recounts the ways in which God used Moses and the forces of nature to redeem an often foolish and rebellious people from their Egyptian enslavement. In clear and simple language, the love of God is seen in his redemptive actions in Egypt as well as in his righteous demands at Sinai.

Thus it lays a solid foundation for understanding all the rest of Israel's history. There is no way to properly understand either the

9

sermons of the prophets or the songs of the poets if we do not first comprehend what God did for and demanded of Israel in Exodus.

Thus Exodus becomes foundational for understanding the ultimate faith of Israel. Their whole awareness of redemption and covenant had its foundation in this book and the events it records. The proper understanding of the meaning of these events is the key to the inner faith and outer rituals of the religion of Israel. For Israel herself, the fundamentals of faith all find their basis in the events of the Exodus/Sinai material.

But there is an even more important reason for studying the book of Exodus. For the Christian, the New Testament understanding of the mission and message of Jesus is largely described in terms and ideas first used in the book of Exodus. If we are going to probe the depths of the full biblical understanding of the work and words of Jesus, we must begin with the ideas and vocabulary of Exodus.

The Nature of the Book of Exodus

The name *Exodus* has come to us through the Latin Vulgate, which in turn received the name from the Septuagint, an ancient Greek translation of the Hebrew Old Testament. (The Septuagint translation was made about the middle of the third century B.C.) In the Hebrew version, a book was named by the opening words of the book. Thus they called this book "These Are the Names of." Such an unhandy and meaningless title readily explains why the later name, *Exodus,* supplanted it.

The question of the authorship of the book is much more difficult. Traditionally it has been called "The Second Book of Moses," but there is no ancient authority for that tradition. Also, in considering the problem, we need to recognize that many of Israel's traditions were probably preserved orally for long periods before they were finally committed to writing. To the modern mind, so used to things of value being put in writing to preserve their accuracy, oral tradition seems quite risky. In the ancient world (as well as in contemporary nomadic societies) such procedures preserved the records with great accuracy. Various parts of the records were likely preserved by different groups. For example, the Levites might have kept records of materials that were of particular importance to them, while other groups preserved their materials of significance.

Moses actually wrote some Exodus material (note Ex. 17:14; 24:4-

7; 34:27). And it is obvious that much more of the material came directly from Moses, for many events are recorded of which no one else could have known. These materials also would have been preserved in both oral and written form by various circles within Israel. Somewhere along the way, perhaps at a time of national crisis, these materials were combined and committed to writing.

The question of authorship is quite complex; however, several factors must be considered. First, the question of the human author has no bearing upon the fact of the divine author. As a part of the Bible, the book is inspired by God and must be so treated as we seek to interpret it. Second, the human author of a particular passage may be of interest, but not of ultimate importance. Third, our basic task is to interpret the message as we have it. The meaning of the actual message is seldom dependent upon who the human author was. That God parted the sea for Israel to cross is of infinitely greater significance than which scribe recorded the event.

For our purposes, we shall assume the following: (1) the human author of the final edition of Exodus is unknown; (2) a significant portion of the material has been handed down orally and in writing from Moses himself; (3) the divine authorship is unquestioned; and (4) it is upon the divine authorship that its authority rests. For those who are interested in a more thorough study of the problems of authorship, the material in *The Broadman Bible Commentary* by Dr. Roy Honeycutt, Jr., will be helpful (vol. 1, pp. 290–297).

The book is a narrative of the historical events that led up to Israel's deliverance from Egypt and culminated in their meeting with God at Sinai, where the covenant was instituted between God and the Hebrew nation. The second major portion is a long list of legal materials that made up the core of the covenant laws by which Israel was bound. A third major section sets forth the regulations for the construction of objects and the ordination of the personnel of worship, coupled with the record of how these were fulfilled.

The Exodus Event

For Israel, the most profoundly significant event in the Old Testament was the experience of the Exodus. The poets and songwriters sang of it and made it a major part of their worship remembrances (Ps. 78; 105; 106; 114; 135; 136). The prophets continually recalled God's deliverance and made it the basis of much of their preaching

(Amos 2:10; 3:1; Hos. 11:1; 12:9; 13:4; Isa. 11:16; Mic. 6:4; 7:15; Jer. 2:6; 7:22-25; 11:4-7; 32:21). The event itself was handled by the people of the Old Testament in much the same way that the life, death, and resurrection of Jesus was treated by the New Testament writers. Thus the book of Exodus became for the Old Testament what the Gospels are for the New. The deliverance was the historical evidence for God's love of Israel.

Further, when God lovingly redeemed them, he established his authority by giving them a covenant. The covenant was the formal seal of what he had done for them. It set forth the terms of his lordship, establishing both his claim to authority and his righteous demands.

Since the divine redemption was an event, actually worked out in history, it had a time and a place. In general, the place is easy to identify. The first part of the story occurred in Egypt, in the northern region of Goshen which had been given to the Hebrews (Gen. 46:28 to 47:12). Further, although there is some debate as to the actual location of Sinai, it must have been in the Sinai Peninsula, on the edge of the Arabian Desert.

The date of the Exodus event has not been as easy for interpreters to agree upon, although there is a growing consensus of opinion that the Exodus occurred during the thirteenth century B.C. According to this reconstruction, the Hebrews would have entered Egypt during the time when a group of foreigners known as the Hyksos were ruling the land. They were Semites, as were the Hebrews. Thus it is easier to understand Joseph's becoming the prime minister, since he was a Hebrew. The Hyksos were later overthrown and a native Egyptian dynasty was established. This was the Eighteenth Dynasty and ruled from a capital about five hundred miles down the Nile from the region of Goshen. These rulers were finally overthrown by those of the Nineteenth Dynasty, who ruled from a capital near Goshen.

Sethi I ruled as a part of this Nineteenth Dynasty from about 1305 to 1290 B.C. He began the construction projects with which the Bible says the Hebrews were involved (Ex. 1:11). He is therefore probably to be identified as the pharaoh of the oppression, the king "who did not know Joseph" (Ex. 1:8). His successor, Ramses II (about 1290–1224 B.C.) would then be the pharaoh of the Exodus. This would fit in well with the facts that an Egyptian monument from the time of Pharaoh Merneptah (about 1224–1211 B.C.) lists Israel as being in the land of Canaan and that archaeological evidence reflects a major invasion and change of culture in Canaan during the last half of the thirteenth century B.C.

The importance of trying to arrive at a specific date for the Exodus is that it helps us understand the actual situation around the recorded events. Regardless of the actual date, the major fact remains that the events around Israel's deliverance were historical. Other nations in the ancient Near East created legends to explain their founding. Israel could point to actual historical events. The God of the Bible was seen by them as one who controlled history. This was and still is extremely important.

The Significance of Exodus

In the Bible, what made an event important was what it meant or what its significance was. Thus, for Israel and for us, the most important feature of the Exodus is what it meant. The divine message made the historical event significant.

We have already noted that Exodus was for Israel what the Gospels are for Christianity. Thus the book is the historical record of God's redemptive activity for Israel. We must clearly recognize that many events of both Israel's and Moses' history, despite their importance to Egypt, to Israel, or to Moses, are not recorded because they were not significant in the redemptive work of God.

The fundamental ideas of Israel's faith all have made their roots in Exodus. It is here that God is first described as one who redeems his people (Ex. 6:6; 15:13). It is in Exodus that God is first described as one who saves his people (Ex. 14:30). It is in Exodus that the first ideas of holiness are set forth in the Old Testament (Ex. 3:5; 15:13; 19:6).

The first clear statement of the nature of God is found in the record of Moses' call (Ex. 3:1 to 4:17). He was presented as one who knew his people's sufferings, kept his promises, and called and sent men to accomplish his purposes.

The basic understanding of Israel's relation to God as his covenant people is set forth in Exodus (19:5-6). Not only did the covenant establish their relationship as God's chosen people; it also laid upon them obligations of obedience and loyalty.

But beyond the Old Testament, the book of Exodus had significance for Jesus. In the Sermon on the Mount (Matt. 5—7), as well as in numerous other places, Jesus showed his awareness and endorsement of Exodus. His last worship service with his disciples was spent in keeping the Passover with his disciples. When he searched for a term to describe what he was doing for them, he called it a new covenant.

Finally, when the early Christians described Jesus as Savior or Redeemer, they were using terms whose basic meaning had been established in Exodus. The church itself is also described in terms first set forth in Exodus (compare 1 Pet. 2:9 with Ex. 19:6). Thus the ultimate significance of Exodus lies in its foundation for the message of the New Testament.

The Name of God

To many students of the Old Testament, the most significant happening in Exodus was the revelation of the meaning of the divine name, YHWH (Ex. 3:13-15). The best evidence available would indicate that the name was originally pronounced as *Yahweh*. The name was originally written without vowels. In postexilic Judaism the name was considered too sacred to pronounce, so another Hebrew word, *Adonai* (meaning Lord), was pronounced in its place. The vowels of the latter word were inserted into the former to remind readers of this fact. When men read it centuries later they did not know this and pronounced it *Yahowah* or *Jehovah*. Obviously there never was such a word as this.

Knowing someone's personal name in those days was equal to knowing his character. It is very likely that the name YHWH was known before Moses' experience and that what he was asking for was an understanding of the nature or character of God. In any event, this was what he was given. He was told that God was the One who was alive, who really existed. But he was also the One who would deliver them, a God of redemption (Ex. 3:16-17). The rest of Exodus was an enlargement of this first revelation of the nature of God as living and redemptive.

From this time forward, the use of the divine name would always remind Israel of God's saving nature and purposes. The name YHWH brought to their minds the same kinds of precious memories that the name Jesus brings to the mind of Christians.

The Message of Exodus

Perhaps the most essential question for us to ask as we begin our study of Exodus is: What is the book about? What is its message to us? There are four possible answers.

First, we might say that the book is about Moses. He is certainly the central figure of the book. Born a slave, he was reared as a favored son in one of the most luxurious royal households of the ancient world. Given an opportunity to take his place of authority within the government, he chose to cast his lot with slaves. Trained in a pagan environment, he propagated a faith that was to change the world. Becoming a murderer in his early manhood, he later set forth one of the most life-respecting law codes the world has ever known. Although Exodus tells us much about Moses, its basic message is not about him.

Second, we might say the book is about Israel. Their drift into slavery and their deliverance from it have been preserved in detail. Both their faithful obedience and their unbelieving rebellion are recorded with care. The book follows their pilgrimage from being a loosely connected group of slaves to becoming the nation of God at Sinai. It reveals both the height of their submission to the covenant and the depth of their rebellion with the golden calf. But even for Israel, the basic message of the book of Exodus was not what happened to them.

Third, some have suggested that the basic message of the book revolves around the tabernacle, priesthood, and worship of Israel. Worship was of great significance to the author of Exodus. To ignore the worship emphasis would be to leave out a major portion of the content. But even this is not the basic message of Exodus.

The fourth answer is the only one that really gets to the heart of the matter. Exodus is about God. It reveals a God who remembers; the past is important to God. Even more important, the God revealed in Exodus is a God who acts. He is involved in history, controls nature, and uses both to accomplish his purposes. He is a God who agonizes with his people and acts to deliver them. He is clearly shown to be a God of grace who chooses men because of his nature and not because of theirs. He is further shown to be a God of righteous demand. He expects an obedient response from his people. Finally, the book shows God as One who loves. The understanding of God which is foundational to biblical faith has its foundation in Exodus. He is what the book is about. All things else are secondary.

Preparations That Point the Way
1:1 to 2:25

For the people of Israel, history was never just a record of events. Nor was it ever merely the retelling of the experiences which they thought were significant. History was important to them because of what God had done in it. This fact shows up clearly in the first section of Exodus. God is seldom mentioned in it, but there is no question but that they understood him as being involved, actually in control. The events recorded were certainly human events, but they were under divine control. These events set the stage for the entire drama of redemption. Their lengthened shadow is seen throughout the rest of Exodus, throughout the entire history of Israel, and even to the end of the New Testament.

The Historical Setting (1:1-22)

Those who came to Egypt (1:1-6).—The book begins by reminding us of the concluding events of Genesis, the entry of Jacob and his family into Egypt. They had come from Canaan in a time of famine and had settled down in Goshen (Gen. 47:1-6). Joseph had arrived in Egypt earlier, having been brought in as a slave following the betrayal by his brothers.

We should focus on the fact that it was a famine which brought the family of Jacob into Egypt. They came for the purpose of preserving life. Their visit to Egypt should have been a temporary visit. When the crisis had passed, they should have moved on. But they did not. The tragic message is that "Joseph died, and all his brothers, and all that generation" (v. 6). The patriarchal age came to an end with the promises of God still unfulfilled.

Selfish fruitfulness (1:7).—The fruitfulness of the descendants of Israel is made emphatic by the fourfold repetition of synonymous expressions. The account is setting forth a bold statement of extreme prosperity. If we are not careful, we may miss a very subtle point. In the popular theology of the people of the Old Testament, prosperity was always assumed to be an evidence of the blessing of God.

Israel was extremely prosperous in Egypt. Almost certainly, Israel's prosperity was assumed by the people to be a testimony to God's blessing. Only one thing was wrong. Goshen was not where Israel was supposed to have settled. It should have been only a temporary stop on the way to Canaan, to the land of God's promise (Gen. 12:7; 13:14-17; 15:7; 35:12; 48:4). However, they seemed to have settled down for a permanent stay. Even though they were prosperous, their prosperity was selfish. They had chosen the easy path of prosperity instead of the way of obedience to God (Gen. 17:6-8; 35:11-12).

The second subtle truth implied here is that Israel's fruitfulness had cost too much. They were about to discover that they had become slaves in Egypt. This had happened without their even being aware of it. The time of peace and prosperity had been purchased at too great a price. Without question, the people had never intended to be disloyal to God or to become slaves to Egypt. But their intention did not matter. The fact was that both happened.

Oppression by forced labor (1:8-14).—It is likely that the "new king" refers to a new dynasty. Most likely this king is to be identified as Sethi I (about 1305-1290 B.C.), the founder of the Nineteenth Dynasty in Egypt. The expression "who did not know Joseph" (v. 8) probably implies far more than just a poor knowledge of history. These native Egyptian kings were attempting systematically to "forget" anything which reminded them of the hated Semitic rulers.

The pharaoh's fear of the Hebrews was not as overwhelming as our translation makes it seem. He was well aware of their numbers and inherent power. But the Egyptians found it fairly easy to control Israel. In fact, without God's help, Israel could not have left the land. The expression might be better translated as: "The people of Israel are numerous and powerful in relation to us." His fear of their potential rather than their actual threat drove him to unreasonable actions.

The assignment of taskmasters to oversee forced laborers from slaves was a standard procedure in Egypt. None of the Egyptians' magnificent building projects could have been accomplished without the Hebrew laborers. The purpose of the oppression of Israel was twofold. First, Egypt retained the economic advantage of having Israel there but removed the potential military threat. Keeping them busy might reduce the danger of revolt, so the king thought. Second, the king also thought that through the sheer exhaustion of the laborers, he could reduce the increasing birth rate. In this he failed. Oppressed peoples have always found their consolations at home.

The two store cities were apparently begun under Sethi I, although they were not named until the time of his successor, Ramses II (about 1290–1224 B.C.). There were many such cities built during this time, so their location cannot be identified with certainty. They were intended either as military supply depots or as centers of trade.

Israel's continued prosperity brought about a feeling of "dread" on the part of the Egyptians. The expression carries a sense of awe. To a superstitious people like the Egyptians, there was something terrifying about the continued fruitfulness of Israel. Fear bred fear until the result was terror.

This resulted in the intensification of the efforts by the Egyptians to make the Hebrews' "lives bitter with hard service" (v. 14). It might be better to translate this as "cruel slavery." Israel had finally discovered that they were slaves in Egypt. But it was too late for them to do anything about it.

Oppression by systematic extermination (1:15-22).—We must remember that the purpose of Pharaoh from the beginning had been to reduce the numbers of the Hebrews. When his first plan failed, he devised a second. He decided to weaken Israel by the systematic extermination of the newborn sons. But his shrewdness was foolishness, for he did not recognize that his real opponent was God.

The names of the midwives mean "Beauty" and "Splendor." The question has been raised as to why there were only two midwives. Either the numbers of the Hebrews were very small, or these were the only two names remembered, or these are heads of guilds or groups of midwives. It seems that the latter is more likely. If this is correct, their names were being used to identify two groups of midwives, a fairly common practice throughout the Old Testament.

The "birthstool" was a hollow stone or a pair of stones upon which women sat or knelt during the process of birth. This method of giving birth was common in the ancient Near East.

We must note that the reason these midwives failed to obey was neither because of their compassion for their people nor because of their deliberate desire to thwart Pharaoh, but because they "feared God" (v. 17). It is worth noting that the supposed stupid and weak slave women outwitted the shrewdness of the Egyptian ruler.

When the king called for an accounting, the midwives responded by saying that the Hebrew women "are vigorous and are delivered before the midwife comes to them" (v. 19). Their explanation has been variously interpreted. It has been suggested that they were deliberately lying. If this is true, we must recognize that their respect for life was greater than their respect for truth. The lie might not have been necessary, but their values were certainly correct. It has also been suggested that they were telling the truth. But if this is correct, we must raise the question as to why they needed midwives in the first place. It has also been suggested that they deliberately delayed arriving until after the birth was completed. On this basis they had interpreted Pharaoh's command quite literally and considered that they were only commanded to kill the boy babies during birth, but not after. In any event, because of their fear of God, they were blessed.

With his plan to relieve the threat of Israel again thwarted, Pharaoh devised a variant upon his second plan. He turned to his own people and commanded them to begin the extermination of all newborn Hebrew sons. The daughters were to be allowed to live to furnish slave labor, concubines, and probably to be available as breeding stock if he were too successful in his plan of reducing the Hebrew numbers. Our translation probably misses the point by wording the command, "you shall cast into the Nile" (v. 22). The Hebrew literally says, "you shall cast in the direction of the Nile." Drowning was cruel but quick. What Pharaoh was proposing was death by exposure, which was slow, sadistic, and even more heartbreaking.

There is a strange parallel between this story and that of Herod's destruction of all newborn sons in Bethlehem (Matt. 2:16). In neither case could Pharaoh or Herod prevent the successful conclusion of God's purpose.

The Birth of Moses (2:1-10)

The focus suddenly shifts from the universal persecution by Pharaoh to the experience of one family within Israel. Although neither God's control and purposes nor Pharaoh's persecution are specifically mentioned in these verses, both are clearly understood as part of the background. An outsider would view these events as perfectly normal. The eye of faith sees them as the hand of God.

Moses' family (2:1).—The names of Moses' parents are not given at this point. They were Amram and Jochebed (6:20). They were both from the family of Levi, which was to become the priestly family within Israel. That Moses should have this lineage was appropriate,

as Moses was the supreme mediator between Israel and God in the
Old Testament.

Moses' birth and early protection (2:2).—This verse would imply
that Moses was the first child of Amram and Jochebed. We discover,
however, that Moses had an older sister (2:4) and an older brother
(7:7). Miriam and Aaron were not unimportant, but the story of God's
redemptive purpose revolved around Moses. Apparently Aaron was
born either prior to or during the time when the midwives were
sparing the children. But Moses was born under threat of death.

The implication of the expression "a goodly child" stands out. To
lose any child would be bad enough, but such a healthy, beautiful
son called forth every effort to preserve his life. For three months
his parents managed to hide him from the Egyptians.

Moses in the basket (2:3-4).—A well baby cries too loudly by the
age of three months to be easily hidden. At this point, Moses' mother
prepared a small basket out of papyrus reeds. The detail of how she
made it waterproof indicated an intimate knowledge of the times
and the specific event. The fact that the basket was placed "among
the reeds at the river's brink" (v. 13) clearly indicates that there was
no intention that the basket should float away. It is also obvious that
the sister's nearby watchcare was a preparation for something important. They were expecting something to happen, and it did.

It would appear that Moses' mother was aware of precisely where
Pharaoh's daughter came to bathe at the river. Her last hope was
that the king's daughter might do exactly what she did. Miriam was
stationed nearby both to protect Moses and to be available when
the need arose. Since a passing soldier could have been attracted
by the baby's cries, Jochebed's plan was dangerous; but there was
no other alternative.

Pharaoh's daughter (2:5-6).—The carefully laid plans of Moses'
mother moved to fruition as the daughter of Pharaoh came down
to the Nile to bathe. Her handmaidens patrolled the river's bank to
attend to her wishes, as well as to protect her. Apparently the basket
had been so situated as to be more visible from the river than from
the shore. This would have given added protection from accidental
discovery by the wrong persons.

Seeing the basket, Pharaoh's daughter sent one of the maids to
get it and bring it to the curious young woman. In the carrying of
the basket, perhaps the baby was jostled and began to cry. Perhaps

the sunlight that streamed into the opened basket also startled him.

Two things stand out here. First, she readily identified the child as a Hebrew. This might have been simply because no one else would have so treated a baby. It is more likely that he was wrapped in a blanket with identifying tribal fringes. Second, the plight of the baby touched the heart of the young woman. She was well aware that her father was engaged in a systematic attempt to execute the male children of the Hebrews. Apparently that neither disturbed nor involved her. But the sight of one helpless baby awoke a distinct response, for "she took pity on him" (v. 6). Here is another human love which God was using to effect his will.

Moses' life preserved (2:7-9).—It was obvious that the baby could not survive without someone to nurse him. This was before the days of bottles, so the only hope was a woman who was producing milk. It is against this background that we must understand Miriam's offer. Although we do not know Miriam's age, she was probably no more than five or six at this time. The knowledge that she would have of the needs of the baby or the availability of a nursing woman would only be what she had been told in advance.

Miriam called Moses' own mother. When she came to the daughter of Pharaoh, the mother was given back her own baby to nourish, to love, and to care for. But now he had the protection of the daughter of the very one who was seeking to kill him.

There seems to be little doubt but that Pharaoh's daughter realized that the woman before her was the baby's mother. There would probably have been few others available. Further, the look of joy in the mother's eyes could not easily have been hidden. Here was a love from woman to woman, a love which crossed social, racial, and legal barriers.

To understand the words "I will give you your wages" (v. 9) as a simple offer to pay is to miss the point altogether. The Hebrew literally means, "I will give you your reward." Moses' mother had struggled against overwhelming odds to save the life of her baby. Pharaoh's daughter recognized this. The reward which was being offered was the life of the child. What more reward could she have had?

"So the woman took the child and nursed him" (v. 9). Once again the plan of Pharaoh had been defeated. God's purposes had been ridiculously (from the world's standpoint) placed in a helpless baby under sentence of death. At no point in the entire story, if we view

it from the human level, would anyone have believed that there was
any hope for Moses. But suddenly, there he was, living in his own
home, cared for by his own mother, and protected by the authority
of the Egyptian royal family.

What was Moses taught during those early days in his own home?
He surely learned from his mother and father of the heritage of his
people and of the promises of God. He was probably also told of his
miraculous deliverance. Maybe his mother even suggested to him
that God, who had specially protected him, must surely have some
great purpose for him. When Moses left his family home to reside
with his adopted mother, he did know he was a Hebrew. He never
forgot this fact.

Moses in the royal palace (2:10).—When he was old enough to
be weaned, he was brought to Pharaoh's daughter. In the ancient
Near East, children were weaned at the age of three or four. Although
this might seem late to us, in those days when a child was weaned,
he had to be able to eat solid, rough food. Therefore Moses' mother
had been able to have him for a fairly long time. Normally a child
was named shortly after birth. Moses had probably been so named.
But when he was officially adopted by Pharaoh's daughter, he was
given a new name, for he had just been "born" into her family. The
name Moses had a double meaning. It meant *son* in Egyptian and
was in common use in names such as Thutmose and Ahmose. That
the name also had a related meaning in Hebrew would have been
considered as having spiritual significance.

The entire episode of Moses' birth and deliverance is a clear indication of God's power to use normal, everyday affairs of life to accomplish
his purposes. Everything that occurred could have been attributed
to normal events or, at best, to coincidence. To the eye of faith, God
was at work in every step of the process.

The Early Manhood of Moses (2:11-22)

We are not told what happened to Moses between the time he
was adopted and the time he began to act for God. But Egypt was
the center of the wisdom of the ancient world at this time. To have
been trained in such an environment would have been similar to a
modern person's being trained on a major university campus. He
had the advantage of the best learning available at that time.

In the palace of Pharaoh he would have been trained in the business of government, including both the common law codes of the ancient Near East and the tasks of administrating them. His governmental training would also have included the nature of international relations, with specific emphasis upon international treaties and covenants.

He would also have been trained in the leadership of armies. This would have involved not merely strategy and tactics, but also the problems of organizing and supplying armies marching in the field.

Each of these matters would serve him well in the tasks which he would be called upon to do for God. The basic training of an Egyptian prince was almost perfect preparation for the man who was to become the leader of God's people. God is a God of economy; he does not waste anything.

The Egyptian murder (2:11-15a).—The Old Testament does not tell us the age of Moses that is reflected by the expression "had grown up" (v. 11). Stephen's sermon reflects a tradition that Moses was forty years old at this time (Acts 7:23). This may be quite accurate, or it may merely be an example of the biblical use of forty to indicate a large number. It is regularly used in this way, so such an interpretation is highly possible. It is also possible that the forty years is used as the equivalent of a generation. This was also fairly common in the ancient world. Regardless, Moses was a mature man at this time.

It is obvious that after all the years of training in the court of Pharaoh, Moses still knew that he was a Hebrew. The Hebrews are acknowledged as "his people" (v. 11). As he looked upon their burdens, he was probably comparing their harsh existence with his life of luxurious ease. The verb translated "looked on" indicates more than mere observation; his emotions were stirred by what he saw. The repetition of the phrase "his people" gives a pointed emphasis to Moses' self-identity with the Hebrews. In both cases, the expression literally means "his brothers." His mother's early training had borne fruit.

From a human standpoint, Moses' actions stand out in the gigantic proportions of a hero, but a hero who was clearly human. His burning passion for justice, his promptness in decision and action, his reckless abandon tempered with careful observation, his blow for deliverance without regard to personal cost—all of these make up the nature of Moses. We shall observe each of these characteristics showing up again.

After killing the Egyptian, he buried him in the sand. That detail clearly establishes the historicity of the account. Bodies were easy to hide in Egypt. If the story had been created by a later writer in

Palestine, he most likely would not have been aware of the sandy nature of Egyptian soil.

In Hebrew the verb "killed" comes from the same root as the earlier verb, "beating." Moses gave him the same which he had been giving the Hebrew, only more so. We must clearly see that it was not Moses' desire to deliver his people which was wrong, for God later utilized that very desire. What was wrong was the way Moses put his desire into action. The end never justifies the means. But Moses thought he was safe, for there had been no witnesses.

His initial blow for his people made him feel the need to visit them again. This time he saw two Hebrews fighting. The same verb used earlier is here translated as "strike." It was obvious that this was a fight to the death. Slavery and oppression had broken down all semblance of social order.

The language addressed to "the man that did the wrong" (v. 13) was law court terminology. The expression indicated that Moses was placing himself in judicial authority over his brothers. The question of the Hebrew struck terror to the heart of Moses, for he became aware that his crime was known. He had forgotten at least two things. First, the Hebrew whom he had delivered the day before was almost certainly going to talk about the event. Second, to the Hebrews, he appeared to be an Egyptian. He would have been dressed and identified as an Egyptian. Moses had apparently thought he would be able to live with his conscience. He could not live with the terror of facing prosecution for his crime.

It was not long before the word actually reached the court of Pharaoh. Moses had now become a wanted man. From all outward evidence, he had totally ruined any opportunity of ever being of any service to God or his people.

Moses' life in Midian (2:15b-22).—Moses' flight from Pharaoh and his arrival in Midian are recorded as if there were no difficulty in making this journey. Midian is traditionally located to the east of the Gulf of Aqaba, on the east side of the Sinai Peninsula and the Wilderness of Paran. Since the Midianites were nomads, their land was never carefully defined and probably overlapped into the Sinai Peninsula at times. Moses' journey obviously required the crossing of several hundred miles of desolate wilderness.

There is no way of knowing why Moses selected this particular region, but there are at least two good possibilities. The first is that this region was outside the normal channels of Egyptian commerce and communication. Thus it would be safer than a flight into the region of Canaan which the Egyptians controlled or into southern Sinai, where the Egyptians had extensive mining operations. A second reason for Moses' choice of Midian might be the fact that these people were also descendants of Abraham (Gen. 25:2).

Wherever there was a well in wilderness regions, there was an oasis. This was a place of rest and refreshment. But it would also be a place where travelers would encamp. We may be confident that when Moses "sat down by a well" (v. 16), he hid himself in the undergrowth nearby. He would not have risked discovery by patrolling Egyptian soldiers.

The plot thickens with the introduction of the "seven daughters" of the priest of Midian. The number seven may have been used symbolically, as sacred, complete. It may also have been quite literal. These girls were caring for the flocks of their father. This would indicate that he was not merely a priest but was probably quite wealthy. Cruel and selfish shepherds waited until the girls had drawn water for the flocks and then drove them away. The noise apparently awoke Moses, who drove the shepherds away. It is obvious that he was a man of both valor and strength. A human touch is added by the fact that Moses, having been victorious, then drew the water for the girls' flocks. He was impressing the girls with his strength and ability.

The girls returned home earlier than usual, to the surprise of their father, Reuel. (The names of their father sometimes give a problem. He is identified as Jethro in Ex. 3:1 and may be also identified as Hobab in Num. 10:29. It was not uncommon for a man to have had two or more names in the ancient Near East. Various traditions probably preserved different names.) The name Reuel means either shepherd of God or friend of God. Either term would have been descriptive of his character and priestly function.

When questioned by their father, the girls reported about their deliverance by an "Egyptian." Probably his mode of dress and hairstyle led the girls to this conclusion. It is also worthy of note that Moses had again been driven to action by injustice and oppression.

For Reuel, his daughters' report was of great significance. A father had the responsibility of getting his daughters well married. A man with several daughters had a real problem. Reuel's immediate reaction was both human and humorous. He was astounded that his daughters could have let such a prize get away. There was also an obligation of hospitality. At Reuel's insistence, Moses was invited to eat. The fugitive from Egypt had found a welcome in the wilderness.

Here is another instance where the biblical writer omitted a great deal of detail, since it was not of significance to God's plan of redemption. Verse 20 ends with Moses being invited to dinner. Verse 21 begins with Moses having already assumed the responsibility of entering Reuel's service and marrying his daughter Zipporah. There is no way of determining the time lapse here, but it is safe to assume that it did not happen overnight.

We know very little about Zipporah. Her name has been interpreted as meaning "Swallow" or "Warbler." It has been less kindly understood as meaning "Twitterer." We may safely assume that Moses settled down to family life and to shepherding the flocks of his father-in-law. To all appearances, his sudden act of passion in Egypt had permanently closed the door of his service to God there.

But there was still a longing for his people in Moses' heart. When his first son was born, he named him Gershom. The very name is related to the Hebrew word for stranger. Although Moses seemed to be permanently settled in Midian, he still felt himself to be a stranger. Everything was going well for him in Midian, but he was in the wrong place and he knew it. There was a note of wistful longing in the name he gave his son. He knew his people needed him.

God's Presence with His People (2:23-25)

These verses draw the opening section to a close and set the final stage for the real drama of redemption. Up to this point, the action has followed Moses. It has almost seemed that God and Israel had passed from the view of the author. But God had always been in control. He had also been as involved in Egypt as in Midian.

Change without change (2:23).—Another indeterminate length of time had passed. The pharaoh who had been oppressing Israel had died. With the new king, however, there had been no change in the oppressive slavery. Moses did not know that the pharaoh had died.

There is no indication that the cries of Israel from their bondage are to be considered as prayers. They may have been praying, but the context makes it seem more likely that they were simply crying out in agony. Either way, their cries were heard by God.

God's awareness (2:24-25).—There is an undertone behind these verses: Although Moses had deserted his people, God had not. He never does. The basic messages here are fourfold, and they reflect a growing intensity.

"God heard their groaning" (v. 24). The Hebrew indicates that God was doing more than merely hearing; he was consciously listening to the cries of his people. He was paying attention to their cries. The Hebrews may not have been aware of this, but it was still true.

"God remembered his covenant" (v. 24). A central feature in the Old Testament is the concept of the covenant relationship between God and the Hebrews. The emphasis was that regardless of Israel's faithfulness or lack of it, God was always faithful. The dependability of God is a central feature of this verse and of the message of Exodus. This is especially noteworthy since the gods of the peoples with whom Israel was in contact were always seen to be capricious and undependable.

"God saw the people" (v. 25). There is more than mere looking implied in this expression. God was carefully looking at the experience of his people. He was examining the situation, grasping its total impact. God is spoken of in very anthropomorphic terms here. But for man there is no way to describe God other than in terms of our experiences.

The last statement brings the climax: "God knew their condition" (v. 25). In the Old Testament, the verb "to know" always refers to something more than mere mental awareness. This verb refers to something learned experientially. It obviously refers therefore to first-hand, personal knowledge. On the human level, it is used of the sexual relation, implying the most intimate kind of knowledge possible (Gen. 4:1). Thus, when "God knew their condition," he knew it because he was experiencing it. God had entered into their suffering, even though they did not know it.

With the acknowledgment that God had entered into their suffering, the stage was set for the beginning of his historical acts of redemption. But they were merely outward manifestations of what God had already begun. For "God heard . . . , remembered . . . , saw . . . , and knew." The Hebrews felt forgotten and alone. But God was with them.

Revelations That Transform Life
3:1 to 7:13

Nothing is ever the same after a man (or a nation) becomes aware of God. The evidence of this truth is clearly seen in this section of Exodus. Before they were aware of God's intervening presence, Moses, Aaron, Pharaoh, Israel, and Egypt were all living normally. Life may not have been good (for Israel it certainly was not), but at least it was dependably steady. After they all became aware of God's presence, everything changed. Even for those like Pharaoh who tried to deny that God had come, life was never the same.

The Call of Moses (3:1 to 4:17)

There is no way of knowing precisely how long Moses had been in Midian when his call came. Even if the numbers in Exodus 7:7 and Acts 7:23 are to be taken literally instead of symbolically, we cannot be sure that he had spent forty years in Midian, for we do not know how long he may have been a fugitive before he arrived in Midian.

The burning bush (3:1-3).—Being a shepherd in that region of the world required extensive wandering, for grass was scarce. Moses' wanderings with Jethro's sheep took him to Horeb.

Horeb and *Sinai* are used interchangeably. They may reflect two different traditions, or they may reflect the fact that Horeb seems to have been a Semitic name, while Sinai was apparently non-Semitic. The suggestion that Horeb may have been the name of a specific peak in the Sinai mountain range is plausible, but there is no other evidence that this was true. The fact that the mountain was located on the "west side of the wilderness" (v. 1) is an evidence of geographic significance. The region would have been east of Egypt and south of Palestine. It would only have been described in this way by someone who was in the region of Midian at the time.

This still does not give us a specific location for the mountain, however. It has been variously located in the central or northern regions of the Sinai Peninsula, in the land of Midian—but east of the Gulf of Aqaba—or in the traditional location in the south central region of the Sinai Peninsula. Since there is no conclusive argument, there does not seem to be any reason to reject the traditional location. The identification of Horeb as "the mountain of God" (v. 1) is noteworthy. This has usually been interpreted as a reading back into the story of what happened there both to Moses and to Israel. This is quite possible and frequently happens in recording events at a later time. However, recognizing that Jethro was a priest in Midian and that he was also a descendant of Abraham (Gen. 25:2), it would appear that he might have had some sort of experience with God in the region. Therefore he might have pointed the mountain out to Moses as "the mountain of God." If this were the case, it might even explain why Moses was in the region. Perhaps the longing in his heart for his people and the memory of his mother's teachings were driving him to encamp near the mountain. But whether it was by accident or choice, Moses drew near to the place and hour of his destiny.

In the appearance of "the angel of the Lord" (v. 2), two important features may be overlooked if we focus too much attention on the miracle of the burning bush. First, there is the question of the identity of "the angel of the Lord." This is not just the typical "angel" of the Bible. Whenever "the angel of the Lord" appears, it is always God who speaks. In some way, he is viewed as an extension of God himself. Second, there is the burning "fire." God regularly reveals himself in fire in the Bible. This is true all the way from Abraham (Gen. 15:17) to Pentecost (Acts 2:3). For Moses, as well as for the men who later heard or read of this event, there was no question but that God was there. The burning bush that was not consumed claimed Moses' attention. The fact that God was there made the event important.

The first revelation (3:4-6).—Several things stand out in this first confrontation of Moses by God. First, God initiated the experience. God came seeking Moses. This is always his way. We do not discover God; he reveals himself to us.

Second, the experience was very personal. God called Moses by name. In the ancient world one who knew your name knew everything about you. There is no way to adequately translate Moses' response, "Here am I" (v. 4). The idea behind Moses' response was that he was standing completely exposed before God. We might paraphrase it by a series of expressions: "observe me; examine me; try me; search me." The response indicated an openness to God's searching presence.

Third, God warned Moses about drawing too near. Sinful man cannot approach a holy God. This must not be understood as a permanent prohibition but as a warning against approaching God too quickly or too lightly. Moses needed to recognize the holiness of God. The ground was not holy of itself; it was holy because God was there.

Fourth, God's self-identification seems strange to us. We would expect the words "I am the God of your fathers" rather than "I am the God of your father" (v. 6). (There is one variant textual tradition which has the plural, but the best evidence indicates that the singular was what Moses understood.) The naming of the patriarchs clearly indicates that God was identifying himself with Moses' forefathers. If we grant that Moses received considerable training at home in his very early years, then this expression comes alive. God was identifying himself as the one about whom Moses had learned in those few years with his own family.

Fifth, when Moses realized who was calling him, he covered his face with his robe. This was done in fear and awe. There is no indication of repentance (or the lack of it) on the part of Moses. At this point, he was simply overwhelmed at God's presence. To read either more or less into this is to miss the point entirely.

The divine call (3:7-12).—The statement of God *to* Moses was directly related to the statement *about* God in 2:24-25. The earlier statement told what God knew and was experiencing in relation to the oppression of the Hebrews. This statement builds upon that and sets forth boldly what God has done and will do in their behalf.

"I have come down to deliver them . . . and to bring them" (v. 8) sets forth the divine condescension and its purpose. God, who has been suffering with his people, is now about to do something about it. He had earlier "remembered" his promises. Now he was about to keep his promises. He was going to bring them out of their slavery in Egypt and into the land of promise. The description of the land as "flowing with milk and honey" (v. 8) is typical of the Old Testament's description of Canaan. Such a land would have been the ideal of an agricultural nation who had to struggle for a harvest.

The list of the peoples who would be found in this land is not intended to be exhaustive (see Gen. 15:19-21; Ex. 3:17; Num. 13:29).

Both the numbers and the names sometimes vary. The list is considered to be typical of the preconquest inhabitants of the land. These peoples included both wandering and settled clans of various racial and national origins.

At this point Moses must have rejoiced at the revelation God had given him. But God was not through. The point of the entire confrontation was reached when he added, "Come, I will send you to Pharaoh" (v. 10). To put this in proper perspective, we must realize two things. Although we know that the pharaoh who had sought Moses' life was dead, Moses did not know this. Second, since this is true, Moses' call was not merely to a very difficult job; as far as he was concerned, it was a call to go back to execution. It is precisely this willingness to die which God demands of all his servants.

We also need to recognize that in Moses' one attempt to furnish leadership to Israel, he had been rejected and rebuffed (2:14). In the light of this background, God's call was completely overwhelming. There is no contradiction between God's announced purpose of delivering Israel and his call of Moses to do the work. We know, if they did not, that the sovereign God regularly accomplishes his purposes through the works of his obedient servants.

The effect of the divine call was catastrophic. It brought Moses face to face with some ultimate questions that anyone must face when he is confronted with God's call.

The first question is: "Who am I?" Before we are too critical of Moses for this response, let us remember that Jesus had something to say about counting the cost (Luke 14:28-32). Moses was forced by the divine call to take personal stock of his skills and abilities. Certainly there was some fear and some reluctance on his part. But there was also a sensible self-evaluation. He was searching himself at two points. He needed to be sure that he could both confront Pharaoh and lead Israel. To fail at either point would be to fail in the mission.

"Who am I? Can I do it?" Both of these are pretty good questions. But God had a good answer. He did not tell Moses how many talents he had or how great he was. Instead, he offered Moses the assurance of the divine presence.

God also told Moses: "This shall be the sign for you." What a sign that was: "You shall serve God upon this mountain" (v. 12). Moses was wanting some physical evidence of success right then. God simply said that the fact that Moses had been called signified ultimate success.

Moses wanted certainty. God was demanding faith. Moses wanted
to be sure he could do the job before he started. God was saying
that he would not know until he had finished.

Since God's answer to the first of Moses' questions had been "But
I will be with you," this brought him to a second fundamental question:
"What kind of a God are you, really?"

God's nature (3:13-22).—There is probably no other passage in the
Old Testament which has been as vigorously studied and as diversely
interpreted as this one. The problems revolve around two issues: What
was Moses asking for, and what was God revealing?

In the Old Testament, to know someone's personal name was to
know something about his character or his nature. Further, a personal
name was revealed only to personal friends or to family members.
In addition, the name of God, Yahweh, was apparently known to
Abraham (Gen. 15:2) and was a part of the name of Moses' own mother,
Jochebed. It may be that these reflect variant traditions, but we must
still deal with the passage and its tradition. There is also the problem
of the very nature of Moses' question. Why did he ask "What?" instead
of "Who?" It would appear that Moses wanted more than just a name.

The problems of the second issue are closely related. Precisely what
was God revealing? The name Yahweh given in verse 15 is not the
same word as that translated "I am" in verse 14, although it comes
from the same root. Was God avoiding Moses' question or answering
it? Was God giving more or less than that for which Moses was asking?

Any solution to the problem must clearly deal with both issues.
Without listing all the proposed solutions, let us consider what seems
to be the best one.

First, Moses was not asking a merely hypothetical question. He
was voicing what he expected to be the natural reaction of his people.
Second, the repeated use of "What?" indicates that Moses was asking
for something more than "Who?" Thus it appears that he already
knew who he was talking to, but was searching for an understanding
of the meaning of the divine name. However, since the name had
not been commonly used before this, it seems that with this revelation,
a major new dimension in the Old Testament understanding of God
was gained. Third, although God does not always outwardly answer
all of man's questions, there is every indication in this passage that
God's answer satisfied Moses. With this as background, the best understanding of this passage may be set forth in the following proposal.

1. Moses was asking not merely for the name of God but for a new understanding of his nature. After all, Israel had suffered for a long time; why was God just then beginning to do something? Further, Moses thought that he was being asked to go to Egypt to die, for he did not know that the former pharaoh had died. He wanted to be sure that the God who spoke to him was worth dying for.

2. The name of God, Yahweh, is related to the Hebrew verb root from which "I am" comes. (The name of Yahweh is in the third person and is that form by which a man might speak to God. The expression "I am" is in the first person and is in the form by which God would speak of himself.)

3. In the Hebrew, verbs have no time connected with them. Time is supplied only by context. God's self-designation as "I am who I am" (v. 14) can be translated in numerous ways. It could be "I am who I was"; "I am who I will be"; "I will be who I was"; "I am what I cause to be" and various other combinations. The name and nature of God was therefore presented as being so full of meaning so that no human expression could ever sum it all up. The nature of an infinite God can never be contained in finite human words. However, several factors stand out. God is consistent. He is the same today as he was yesterday or will be tomorrow. This would have been a startling revelation, for the gods of the surrounding peoples were capricious, inconsistent, and undependable. Moses was being told that man can rely upon God and his unchanging nature.

Closely related to this, the expression implies that wherever God was—in Canaan with Abraham, in Egypt with Israel, or in Sinai with Moses—he was the same. He speaks of the same matters in different places and to different generations. Next, Moses was being told that God was one who really existed. Other gods may be spoken of and worshiped, but the God of Israel "is." The word also implies that God is the Creator, the One who causes to be.

4. Since the God of the Hebrews has a personal name, he is a person. Neither Moses nor Israel ever considered God as some great "force" or "power." He was always met as a person with personal characteristics.

Having established his nature and identity with Moses, God began to spell out in detail what Moses' task was to be. It was initially to be a mission to the people of Israel in the persons of their leaders. He was commanded to "Go . . . gather . . . say" (v. 16). God had a message for Israel that Moses was to deliver.

Then Moses was told that these leaders were to accompany him to Pharaoh. This was his ultimate mission. He was to demand that Israel be granted freedom to make a journey to serve their God. At this point the whole future story was outlined for Moses. He was warned that Pharaoh would not accept his demand without the intervention of God. He was told of the "wonders" which God was going to perform. He was also told of the ultimate victory that God would have over Egypt.

It did not really take a divine revelation for Moses to know that Pharaoh would not welcome his demand. No despot would give up cheap labor willingly. Neither did it require much of a revelation for Moses to know that if victory was to come, it would have to come by God's power.

Apparently Moses was not really thinking about God's commission. He was hearing the words; but their real impact escaped him, for he was later surprised when things became so difficult. The details included here may have been a later reading back into the story of what actually happened. It is equally as likely that Moses' mind was hanging upon the one unmentioned fact: As far as he knew, he was still a wanted man in Egypt. He may have been thinking about the cost of God's demand.

Evidences of God's presence (4:1-9).—Moses was convinced that he had a sufficient knowledge of God and his nature to make the mission possible. We should emphasize the word *possible,* for in no way did Moses yet believe that the mission was practical. He raised the question as to how he would convince the people of Israel of the authenticity of his mission. It was a legitimate question. Consider the fact that he had been raised in the court of Pharaoh, was a murderer with a price on his head, had dwelt in Midian for many years, and had a Midianite wife and sons by her; and you will readily see why Moses might not have expected his people to believe him.

God gave him three signs to perform. The first was the transformation of his rod, the second of his hand, and the third of the water from the Nile. Jesus later refused to perform such signs to authenticate his own mission (Matt. 12:39). However, such signs were frequently performed in the Old Testament. When Jesus came, he himself was the sign.

In seeking to understand this passage, we must first recognize the nature of a sign. A sign points to a meaning beyond itself and has no value if its meaning is not understood. This is true whether we are speaking of a biblical sign or a street sign. So if we get bogged down in discussing the nature of these signs, we are likely to forget to search for their meaning.

It was obvious that the signs were of divine origin. Without pressing for a detailed analysis of their specific nature, it is sufficient for faith to recognize that here was something which God did. The signs were to be the outward evidence of the presence of God with Moses.

Moses' excuses (4:10-17).—Moses' first two responses to God ("Who am I?" and "What is your nature?") can be viewed as legitimate. His third response, "They will not believe me" (4:1), was a legitimate problem, but exposed Moses' lack of faith in God's promise. He had been told, "They will hearken to your voice" (3:18). With this present section we clearly move into the area of excuses instead of reasons. Moses did not wish to do what God had called him to do. He was searching for excuses and exposing a real lack of faith.

His excuse, "I am not eloquent" (v. 10), is never stated to be false. In fact, there is every indication that it was true. He felt unable to do what God wished. But he became critical of God when he stated that he was the same as he was before God had come. He was wrong. God had made a difference.

We must recognize that the Bible does not hide Moses' humanity. Indeed, this fact helps us identify with him. God did not indicate that Moses' estimate of his personal abilities was incorrect. Instead, Moses was blamed because his excuses indicated a real lack of faith.

God's response to Moses in verse 11 indicates a certain amount of exasperation. The implication of the divine questions was that the God who has made man knows what he can do. God never calls us to do what we cannot do. God's command to Moses became quite emphatic. It would be better translated as: "Now as for you, you go; and as for me, I will be with your mouth." Moses was being told that his responsibility was to obey, while God's responsibility was to empower. Moses needed to take care of his responsibility and to leave God's responsibility to God.

Moses' fifth response is clearly nothing more than an excuse. No reason is given. There is simply the bold statement, "Send, I pray, some other person" (v. 13). God's patience had been exhausted, and his anger was aroused by Moses' reaction.

At this point God told Moses of the coming of Aaron (see 4:27). Perhaps Aaron was coming to tell Moses of the death of the pharaoh who had sought his life. Whatever the reason, the fact is that Aaron was available. Moses could have done the job God called him to do. By his refusal, he lost some of the honor he might otherwise have had. Further, the presence of Aaron at this point certainly had some bearing in the later sin with the golden calf (Ex. 32).

It is important to note two things about the relationship between Moses and Aaron. First, they were brothers, with Aaron being the elder. This family relationship must always be kept in mind in their future dealings with each other. Under normal conditions, the elder would have been the leader. But this was to be reversed here.

Second, Aaron was to be a "mouth" to Moses, and Moses was to be as God to Aaron. This is important for the Old Testament understanding of the messengers to God. Aaron was given no message. He was merely to be the mouthpiece through whom Moses was to speak. God in no way let Moses out of his call or commission. He might not go back to speak, but he was going back. The time for discussion had come to an end. Moses either had to obey or refuse. If he refused, it would be done with the clear understanding that no excuse was left. Moses was not in a position to negotiate.

God's final word in the call narrative was the commission to take in his hand the rod by which he was to perform his signs. For Moses, this was to be the symbol of God's presence and power. Sadly, he later seemed to rely too much upon it (Num. 20:11-12).

The Mission of Moses (4:18 to 5:21)

The journey begun (4:18-26).—Following his final surrender, Moses returned to Jethro. This was necessary in order to get the flock back, as well as for Moses to get his wife and family together. It may seem strange to us that Moses asked Jethro's permission to return to Egypt. In the patriarchal family life of the ancient Near East, the patriarch was the absolute head of the household, including the in-laws. We may wonder why Moses did not tell Jethro the real reason for his wishing to go back to Egypt. The expression "see whether they are still alive" (4:18) simply means, "see how they are getting along." We probably have here an illustration of the fact that men find it easier to talk of human relations than of divine ones. Jethro readily granted Moses permission without additional inquiry.

We do not know what transpired in Moses' life between verses 18 and 19. Moses may have been slow in getting ready for the journey. He was certainly fearful as he pondered the fact that he was still a "wanted man" in Egypt. At this point God came with a chiding encouragement, telling Moses that those who had been seeking his life were dead. What a relief this must have been to Moses. He had finally gotten to the point that he was willing to die, but he surely did not wish to do so. With this burden lifted, Moses sped his departure. He apparently thought that there were going to be no other difficulties. In this he was wrong. The worst was yet to come.

As Moses began his journey, he surely began to ponder what was going to happen when he arrived in Egypt and attempted to do what God had commanded. God spoke to him through these processes, reminding him of the power that had been given him. Moses was never to forget that God was the miracle worker.

In the expression "I will harden his heart" (v. 21), we are brought face to face with what some have found to be a problem. Several things stand out as we consider this. Exodus speaks of God hardening Pharaoh's heart, Pharaoh hardening his own heart, and simply of the fact that his heart was hardened, without citing its source. What, then, was happening to Pharaoh? God was pressuring Pharaoh, squeezing his heart, forcing him to make a decision. God knew what the decision was going to be, but the decision was clearly Pharaoh's. We should also note that this was no problem to the men of the Old Testament. It sometimes becomes a problem for us since we tend to think theoretically, while they thought practically.

Furthermore, here in the beginning of the experience, God was laying the foundation for the final confrontation in the death of the firstborn sons of Egypt. This is the first time that Israel is referred to as God's firstborn son. In addition, we see here laid out the judicial foundation for the later visitation of death. If Pharaoh tried to keep Israel away from God, which would be spiritual death, God would separate the Egyptians from their firstborn sons. We need not plead that this is beneath the love and mercy that Jesus revealed. Of course it is. But in the ancient world men did not believe that gods were or needed to be just. Moses was being taught that God was just. It was a giant step in the process of revelation.

Although we have only been told of the birth of one of Moses' sons, by this time he had two (v. 20). Both of them, along with Zipporah, set out with Moses on the way back to Egypt. At this point we are confronted with a very strange passage (vv. 24–26). At an oasis where they encamped along the way, we are told that "the Lord met him and sought to kill him" (v. 24). Although some commentators see the "him" as referring to Moses' firstborn son, it seems more likely that this refers to Moses. But why should the God who has called Moses now try to kill him when he finally set out in obedience? Without detailing the many fanciful explanations offered, let us consider several ideas.

In the Old Testament illness is frequently described as having been sent from God, for all things ultimately came from God. Further, the fact that one or both of Moses' sons had not been circumcised probably indicates that Moses had not only neglected this, but had neglected other parts of his religious heritage as well. The neglect of circumcision would just have been a symptom of a more serious problem. When Moses fell ill he began searching his conscience to see if there were any obvious explanation, and there was. Although not all illnesses may be connected with sin, the fact that some are so connected is indisputable.

Too weak to perform the rite himself, he had to have Zipporah do it. When she had finished, she flung the piece of skin at Moses' feet in disgust. The exact meaning of the name which she called Moses has been lost in the mists of time. It apparently was a part of an ancient ritual of circumcision that has now been lost. At any rate, Moses had failed to fulfill the Abrahamic covenant (Gen. 17:23; 21:4) and could not proceed in his service of God without doing so.

Israel's reaction to Moses' message (4:27-31).—In the historical situation, God's command to Aaron must have come somewhat earlier. But two events that happened at the same time must be written one after the other. For our purposes, God was at work both in Egypt and in Midian. Moses had already been told that Aaron was coming to meet him (4:14); now the story was being told from Aaron's standpoint. As Aaron journeyed from Egypt, Moses was coming from Midian. They met at the mountain of God. Sinai was between Midian and Egypt.

Upon their meeting, "Moses told Aaron all the words of the Lord . . . and all the signs" (v. 28). Moses apparently found it easier to tell Aaron about God's revelation than he had been able to tell Jethro. This may have been due to the fact that he had been given an authority over Aaron which he did not possess with Jethro. We are told nothing of Aaron's reaction or response to all this. Neither are we told of the rest of the journey. The stage had now been fully set for the mission to Israel in Egypt, and the scene abruptly shifts there.

When the two brothers arrived in Egypt, they gathered the elders together. There was no way by which Moses and Aaron would have addressed all the people of Israel—not even just the men. So they turned to those men who would have been the clan and community leaders. Israel (and most other nations of the ancient Near East) placed a premium on age. The experience and wisdom gained by mere survival gave an acknowledged place of leadership to these men.

Aaron began his first efforts as Moses' spokesman when he addressed the elders. He passed on the message of God. Our biblical text is unclear as to whether Moses or Aaron performed the signs which God had given Moses. Almost certainly it was Moses who did so, since there is no indication that Aaron had been given this power.

In response to this message and these signs from God, "the people believed" (v. 31). We must raise the question about to whom this expression refers. Was it just the elders who believed, or was it all the people of Israel? We cannot answer with certainty; but given the normal operation of the community, the elders would have passed on the message, and the national response would be reported here. It is worth noting that the people did not give Moses any of the problems that he had feared in Egypt.

The people of Israel had long felt that God had forgotten them. Suddenly, here came Moses and Aaron with a message to the contrary. God knew their sufferings and was coming with Moses and Aaron to do something about them. This message served to call the people to worship God. Moses was completely accepted as the new leader, and the people rejoiced in God's deliverance.

The demand rejected by Pharaoh (5:1-14).—Fresh from the ready acceptance of the Hebrew people, Moses and Aaron turned to the major task—meeting with Pharaoh. We are not told whether they went to the palace and were granted an audience with the king or whether they confronted him in the fields as he went about his affairs. It is more likely that they confronted him out in the open.

The straightforward demand of God was flung at Pharaoh: "Let my people go" (v. 1). Although the translation does not reflect it, the Hebrew word for "feast" implies a religious festival at the end of a pilgrimage. It would have been obvious, then, that a significant journey was being anticipated from the very beginning.

The demand was thrust at Pharaoh as having come from "the Lord (Yahweh), the God of Israel" (v. 1). Israel was a national or tribal identity. To recognize "the God of Israel" would have been to acknowledge that these slaves had an identity and dignity which he would not grant.

His response was expressed with arrogance and contempt. "I do not know the Lord, and moreover I will not let Israel go" (v. 2). "To know" meant "to have experienced." Pharaoh was surely telling the truth here, for he had had no experience with God. But that was about to be changed.

Following Pharaoh's rejection of their demand, Moses and Aaron responded with a gentler request. This was more polite in wording, but the nature of the demand was no less. With the Hebrew sense of numbers, the "three days' journey" is probably not to be understood literally, but was intended to describe a "complete journey" or a "sufficient journey." Pharaoh clearly understood this demand to be just as great as the earlier one. Furthermore, since Pharaoh had refused to speak of the God of Israel, Moses identified him as "the God of the Hebrews" (v. 3). This was equivalent to saying, "the God of your slaves." Moses was not going to allow Pharaoh to be able to plead that he had not understood.

Pharaoh's ultimate reaction to Moses' demand was one of total unbelief. He who does not know God seldom understands the discussion of God by those who do. Since Pharaoh could not (or would not) comprehend the spiritual dimensions of Moses' experience, he sought to find a natural, normal reason to explain it. His immediate assumption was that his slaves did not have enough work to do. Having idle time on their hands, so he thought, had given rise to their foolish ideas about going off to serve their God.

Confident in his own analysis of the situation, Pharaoh took steps to increase their labor. The Hebrew slaves were being used to make bricks for Pharaoh's building projects. These were sun-dried mud bricks. They were considerably larger than the bricks with which we are familiar. They were made of clay which had been thoroughly mixed with chopped straw to bind it together. Up to this point the Egyptians had furnished the straw, and the Hebrews had done the mixing and the molding. Pharaoh demanded that the Hebrews should now have to go and gather their own straw while still turning out the same number of bricks each day. This would have been equivalent to having to work an extra shift daily.

The order was passed down, and the workload increased immediately. The Hebrews had to go farther and farther afield, trying to find sufficient straw. They were also reduced to using stubble as a poor substitute. But with all of their increased labors, they were unable to maintain their daily production of bricks. When this happened, the taskmasters (who were Egyptians) began having the foremen (who were Hebrews) beaten.

Moses had come demanding that Pharaoh surrender to the will of God. Pharaoh had refused, just as God had warned that he would do. But it seems that both Moses and Israel were unprepared for the manner in which Pharaoh reacted. Not only did Pharaoh deny the request; he tried to make them forget their need to obey God.

Israel turns against Moses (5:15-21).—As a result of Moses' presentation of the demands of God, the oppression of his people had been intensified. Instead of their receiving deliverance from the burdens of slavery, the grinding, binding nature of the slavery had been made even more real. At this point, the Hebrew foremen "cried to Pharaoh" (v. 15). This is the same word used earlier of their cry to God (2:23). There God had heard their cry and had begun to do something about it. Pharaoh refused to listen to them.

The Hebrews clearly laid the problem before Pharaoh when they placed the burden of guilt upon their overseers, Pharaoh's "own people" (v. 16). As they should have expected, they found no sympathy from the king of Egypt. The Bible indicates that he was almost ranting as he turned them back to their labors. At this the foremen realized just how difficult their situation had become. They had received no relief from Pharaoh. They could see no way in which Moses and Aaron had helped them. Neither did they see any real help coming from God. Their labors had been increased to an amount which they could not produce. They were being beaten for their failures. Surely, from a human standpoint, the situation looked hopeless.

As the foremen were returning from their audience with Pharaoh, they met Moses and Aaron, "who were waiting for them" (v. 20). Moses and Aaron were obviously waiting to hear the results of the foremen's pleading with Pharaoh. Since there had been no relief from Pharaoh, the foremen turned their hostility upon Moses and Aaron.

Thus a side effect of Pharaoh's strategy was that he had caused a division among the leaders of Israel. The real enemy was Pharaoh and Egypt, but the leaders turned on Moses.

"The Lord look upon you and judge" (v. 21), said the foremen to Moses and Aaron. This is a typical expression of righteous indignation from one who thinks he is suffering innocently. It was an implied accusation against Moses. One of the risks of leadership is that when things go wrong, the blame is usually placed upon the leader.

The expression "you have made us offensive" literally means "you have made us stink." They saw themselves as having become loathsome in the presence of the Egyptians. Because of this loathing, they rightly felt that Pharaoh and his people were out to destroy them.

The accusation lodged against Moses was tragic. He was being told that if he had not begun trying to do God's will, there would have been no problems. The struggle to obey God is never easy; but it is always best, even when it is costly. Israel's problem was that they had assumed that obeying God would be easy. They had been wrong.

God's Call Reaffirmed (5:22 to 6:13)

Moses had come back to Egypt in obedience to God. Both Pharaoh and Israel knew this claim. But Pharaoh did not believe it, and Israel had quit believing it. In this passage even Moses begins to question it. Everyone involved underestimated the power of God.

God's encouragement for faltering faith (5:22 to 6:1).—Moses' reaction to the rebuff of his people gives a real insight into his nature. His humanity shows through in his faltering faith. Not only had God done nothing, as far as he could see; things had gotten worse. But Moses also shows the quality of his prayer life. In contrast to Israel, Moses did not lose his faith, even though he could not see what God was doing. So he took his questioning doubt to God.

Many of the great men of the Old Testament had doubts (Jeremiah, Job, and Habakkuk). The Bible never condemns them for this. But they all characteristically took their doubts to God. Great faith seems to grow on doubts honestly admitted and exposed to God.

Moses also expressed his self-concern and his sense of aloneness. "Since I came . . . thou hast not delivered" (v. 23) expressed too much attention to his own actions and too little awareness of what God was doing.

One of the secrets of Moses' greatness may be found in his prayers.

He never mouthed pious platitudes but exposed his real feelings and problems to God. We should pay particular attention to several qualities of his prayers. Here the quality is one of honesty. He spoke to God in an accusing voice, but he was seeking a real answer.

God's response might be considered surprising. He did not rebuke Moses for his doubt or accusation. Neither did he rebuke Israel for their lack of faith. His statement was one of encouragement: "Now shalt thou see what I will do" (v. 1, KJV). Pharaoh had answered Moses with a show of authority and oppressive power. To this, God had replied that they were about to see what real power was.

The call renewed (6:2-9).—In further response to Moses' accusation that God had not done anything, God replied with a renewal of the divine call. In essence, his answer to Moses was, "Remember who I am." The call as restated here should be read in parallel with that in chapter 3. They are variants carrying the same basic information. However, there are some differences. The major difference, of course, is that this is placed in a setting following Moses' return to Egypt.

"I am the Lord" (v. 2) is simply, "I am Yahweh." Here no explanation of the meaning of the divine name is given. None was needed. Moses had been questioning where God was and what he was doing. God's response was a reaffirmation of the very fact of his existence. "I am the One who is."

Beyond this, God reaffirmed his historical relation to the patriarchs. But here there is a difference in the revelation. The added statement that he had been known earlier as "God Almighty" (*El Shaddai*, in the Hebrew) indicated a difference in the way they had known him and the way he was going to be known in the Exodus. The earlier emphasis had been upon the power of God. The new emphasis was to be upon his presence, his existence.

"By my name Yahweh I did not make myself known to them" (author's translation). Given the Hebrew understanding of names, this statement does not necessarily mean that before Moses no one knew the name Yahweh. It may mean that they did not understand the nature of God that the name revealed. There are several instances prior to Moses' time where the name of Yahweh is used in the Old Testament (Gen. 15:2,8; 16:2; 24:31; 38:13). Although it is possible that these uses of the divine name may have been the reading back of a variant tradition, it is also clear that the real understanding of the nature of God took a major step forward in the Exodus experience.

One of the more significant items in the renewal of Moses' call was the reference to the covenant. The concept of God's promise to give Israel the land and the fulfillment of that promise serves as the central focus of Genesis through Joshua. The covenant concept involved several distinct features. (1) God related himself to his people through his promises of grace. (2) God could be depended upon to remember and keep his promises. (3) The people of God were called upon to remember God's promises and to trust him to fulfill them. (4) The covenant gave them hope for the future. All of these are wrapped up in the single word *covenant*.

The renewal of Moses' call also contained a restatement of God's awareness of Israel's sufferings as well as his promised deliverance. It added a new dimension: "I will redeem you with an outstretched arm and with great acts of judgment" (v. 6). This is the first time in the Old Testament that God speaks of "redeeming" anyone. The concept has been made rich by the New Testament description of Jesus as our Redeemer. This particular term comes from a Hebrew word which meant "kinsman-redeemer." The redeemer was the closest of kin, the next of kin. The responsibilities inherent in this relationship involved taking a kinsman's widow when he had died childless and producing offspring which would carry on the family name (Ruth 2:20; 3:13). Thus the redeemer was to produce fruit.

He was also responsible for rescuing his kinsmen from bondage (Lev. 25:48-49). He was further responsible for redeeming land (Lev. 25:25; Jer. 32:1-15), keeping this gift of God within the family. Further, it was the kinsman-redeemer's responsibility to avenge the death of his kinsmen (Num. 35:19; Deut. 19:6). Through the covenant relation, God had established himself as the next of kin for Israel. Through the New Covenant, Jesus has done the same for us. All the beauty and depth of meaning that the term "Redeemer" later holds is an outgrowth of this first mention.

As a part of God's redemptive activity in behalf of Israel, he promised, "I will take you for my people, and I will be your God" (v. 7). The end result of his gracious acts will be that Israel will "know" Yahweh. This means that they will have experienced God in his redemptive activity. Their knowledge of God will not be intellectual but experiential. All of his actions were summed up in his vow to fulfill the ancient promises and bring them to the land of Canaan.

Moses obviously found encouragement from this reaffirmation of his call and of the divine promises. His own faith renewed and his doubts eased, he returned to his people with the message of God. Although Aaron is not mentioned here, we can safely assume that he was still Moses' spokesman. This time, however, when the message of God was laid before the people, "they did not listen" (v. 9). Their hopes had been raised and dashed. Thus it was more difficult to get them to believe again. In the beginning, they had expected it to be too easy. In the end, they expected it to be too difficult.

The recommissioning (6:10-13).—Apparently, after the people of Israel refused to hear Moses' renewed message, his own confidence was shaken again. At least he did not immediately go to Pharaoh to renew his plea. Thus God gave him a new commission.

At this point Moses began again to argue with God. It is no wonder that Moses lacked confidence. Since his own people had refused to heed him, how could he expect Pharaoh to pay any attention? The expression "uncircumcised lips" seems to refer to Moses' inability to speak, not to his unworthiness to speak.

We must note that God did not rebuke Moses here, either. God understands human weaknesses and frailties. Instead, God gave Moses encouragement. A new charge was laid upon Moses to speak both "to the people of Israel and to Pharaoh king of Egypt." But his charge was also to "bring the people of Israel out of the land of Egypt" (v. 13). It may have been that Moses had become so engrossed with what he was to say that he needed to be reminded that he was also supposed to be doing something. He needed to discover that involvement in action so absorbs our minds that we forget our fears.

The Mission Renewed (6:14 to 7:13)

The religious heritage (6:14-27).—To our modern readers, the insertion of a genealogy at this point is very distracting. It was not so to the ancient Hebrews. It was important for them that the credentials for the God-called leaders should be established. Obviously, this is not a full genealogy. It begins with the three eldest sons of Jacob, continuing until it gets to the family of Levi. Then it follows the line of Levi until it gets to Aaron and Moses (v. 20). The order listed here is that of birth, for Aaron was Moses' older brother.

It is also interesting that as the author follows the line onward, it is the family of Aaron which is listed. This may have been done since Aaron was the older. Family leadership usually passed through the line of the older son. It may, however, indicate the priestly interest of the author at this point. Moses was the great prophet, lawgiver, and spokesman for God. But it was through Aaron that the priestly family in Israel was born. Thus the author may have been establishing not merely the credentials of Aaron and Moses, but also the credentials of the entire priestly line.

It is obvious from verse 26 that the fundamental interest here was establishing the position of Aaron and Moses. "These are the Aaron and Moses" (v. 26) to whom the Lord had spoken. It was important for Israel to know that God had been preparing the family line all along. God had not been caught napping by Israel's experience in Egypt. He had been preparing even before they went into Egypt.

It is further important for us to realize the historical continuity set forth here. The older brothers were the leaders of the family when they came into Egypt. It was Moses and Aaron who were to be the leaders when they went out of Egypt. With all of the earlier emphasis upon God's covenant and promises, it was important to make it very clear that those who were about to come out of Egypt were the descendants of those who had received these promises. God does not lose track of his people.

God's purpose in Moses' life (6:28 to 7:7).—Since the insertion of the genealogical table broke the continuity of the narrative, the author returned to it by retelling part of what had gone before. Several of the events were being retold to refresh the reader's mind.

The statement concerning Moses' and Aaron's relationship to each other and to Pharaoh is important for the light it sheds upon the Old Testament understanding of the nature of a prophet. Yahweh made Moses "as God to Pharaoh" (v. 1). He was given an authority over Pharaoh. As we have seen earlier, Aaron was to speak Moses' words to the king of Egypt. These words had an immediacy about them, confronting Pharaoh and demanding response from him. This is precisely the office of the prophet. He was to be God's spokesman to a historical situation, demanding response from those to whom he spoke.

We are also told again of God's hardening of Pharaoh's heart (v. 3). The difficulties of the task and Pharaoh's refusal either to hear Moses or to heed the divine "signs and wonders" (v. 3) are clearly spelled out again. The promise of ultimate deliverance was also repeated to Moses.

The new dimension in this retelling begins with the statement of the divine purpose, that "the Egyptians shall know that I am the Lord." God's purpose was more than just redeeming Israel or keeping his promise. His purpose was also that Egypt should learn by experience the sovereign nature of the living God. Redemption is always a witness to the nature and power of God.

Moses and Aaron began again to fulfill the divine mission. The revelation of the purpose of God seemingly gave them renewed strength for the task. The author gives the ages of both of these men to nail down to actual history the events which he has recorded.

God's power in Moses' hand (7:8-13).—In making their return to Pharaoh, Moses and Aaron were told to perform one of the three signs which had been given them in Egypt. They had probably earlier performed all of the signs before the Hebrew elders (4:30). In the presence of the Egyptians, the turning of water into blood actually became the first plague. The sign of the skin illness may have been the later plague of boils, or else it was not performed at all.

Moses was warned that Pharaoh would demand to see some demonstration of God's power as proof of his claims. The "miracle" spoken of here is the same Hebrew word which is translated as "wonders" in 7:3. The word does not necessarily refer to what we mean by a miracle. It is not always a supernatural event. It can also be some unusual event or a normal event with an unusual meaning. In the Old Testament, a miracle is frequently supernatural. But it may also be something quite natural that became a miracle because it happened at the right place at the right time and there was someone present who could point to the act of God in it.

As we seek to understand what happened in this miracle, we must consider several facts. First of all, it certainly sounds supernatural from our standpoint. Second, the Egyptian sorcerers and wise men were able to duplicate it. Either their duplication was some form of sleight of hand, or else it was not a supernatural event. There is no biblical evidence to demonstrate that the Egyptians were miracle-workers. Third, and most important, the serpent from Moses' rod "swallowed" those of the Egyptians. The word translated "swallowed" seems to have referred to gulping. This would be the typical way of describing a reptile's swallowing. At any rate, the power of the God of Moses was able to overcome the power of the gods of Egypt.

Pharaoh was not impressed by the initial sign, which the Egyptians had seemingly matched. He was not impressed that the Egyptians' serpents had been devoured. His heart remained hardened.

Everything was just as God had warned Moses that it would be. God's foresight into these events in no way means that Pharaoh was not free to make his own choices. He refused to hear Moses, just "as the Lord had said" (v. 13). But he was the one refusing. No one forced him to that decision.

Thus the stage had been set for the main confrontation. God had revealed himself to Moses and Aaron—and through them to Israel, to Pharaoh, and to Egypt. Because of this revelation, the situation had changed. Not one of them would ever be the same again. When God involves himself in any situation, everything is always different.

Confrontations That Demand Decision
7:14 to 13:22

This section of Exodus is one of the most skillfully written narratives in the entire Old Testament. As a fascinating story, it makes exciting reading. The basic plot is simple: A series of catastrophic events befell Egypt, resulting in the liberation of the Hebrew slaves. But carefully woven throughout this basic plot are three subplots, and each must be followed if we are to understand the whole.

The first of the subplots is the actual confrontation between Yahweh, the God of Israel, and the gods of Egypt. Probably no other nation in the ancient world had as many gods and goddesses as Egypt. The plagues which came upon Egypt were neither God cruelly playing with the helpless Egyptians nor merely demonstrations of the awesome power of Israel's God. They were direct and specific confrontations between the God of Israel and the gods of Egypt, and in every instance Yahweh was victorious.

The second subplot focuses our attention upon the changing reactions of the leaders of Egypt. At the beginning, they took the entire matter rather lightheartedly. But this attitude gradually began to change, at least on the part of some of them. More and more of the Egyptians began to take Moses and his God seriously.

The third subplot directs our attention toward Moses. He was faced with constant pressures to compromise, to settle for less than that which God demanded. His loyalty to God, his perseverance to his task, and his concern for ultimate victory shine forth through the story.

God's Signs and Wonders (7:14 to 10:29)

The various words used to describe the plagues are all significant. They are called "signs and wonders" (7:3), as well as being described by verbs meaning "I will plague" (8:2) or "I will strike" (7:17). The first words point beyond the actual event to its meaning, while the latter ones focus upon the sudden intensity of each plague. Although "plague" is probably not a completely accurate description of all of the events, the word has become so much a part of our vocabulary that we shall continue to use it. But it is imperative that we remember that the events were far more than plagues. If we miss the fact that they were "signs and wonders," we shall have missed their major significance.

A second feature that we need to consider before turning to the actual content of each plague is the ethical or moral questions involved. Serious ethical objections have been raised to the way Egypt was treated in these plagues. Of course, the revelation of the Old Testament was progressing toward the ultimate revelation of God in Jesus Christ. If this were not so, we would not have needed a New Testament at all. On the other hand, it should be obvious that to deliver Israel, God must use his power to do it. Such acts as would free Israel had to be oppressive to Egypt. The men of the Old Testament were able to see God's loving, redemptive purpose at work, even in acts of violence. This may not eliminate the moral problem which some have, but it points up the fact that the situation is not as simplistic as some people think it is.

Plague 1: the transformation of the water (7:14-24).—One of the chief gods in Egypt was the Nile River. Egypt received very little rainfall. The agriculture of the land was almost totally dependent upon the Nile for water. Each year the melting snows in the headwaters caused the Nile to flood. When it flooded, it deposited a layer of very fertile alluvial soil, and it also raised the ground water table. After it receded, the fields were easily irrigated by diverting part of the Nile's waters into a network of ditches and canals. Thus the Nile itself was the source of the fertility and water which made life possible in that arid land. Furthermore, the very regularity of the annual flood added to the awe with which the Egyptians viewed the Nile. Thus it is easy for us to understand why they considered the Nile as a major god. Without the Nile there would have been no Egypt. The first plague, then, was a direct confrontation between the Nile as a god of Egypt and the God of Israel.

We should note that the plagues began to come because, as God said, "Pharaoh's heart is hardened" (v. 14). The developing confrontations intensified the hardness of Pharaoh's heart, but it was hardened from the beginning.

The fact that Moses and Aaron were to meet Pharaoh as he was going to the water may be significant. It is quite possible that it was about the time for the Nile to begin its annual flood. Pharaoh and his counselors may have been going to check on it. At the very time when the king was expecting the Nile's life-giving flood, it was going to be turned into something foul and useless.

Moses was commanded to tell Pharaoh that the plague was coming. He was also told to say it was coming because "you have not yet obeyed" (v. 16). By his failure to act, Pharaoh had shown that he did not recognize God's sovereignty. It would have been surprising for an Egyptian king to have recognized the existence or authority of the God of an enslaved people. But he was going to learn (v. 17).

Moses and Aaron did as God had commanded, striking the Nile with the rod of God, "and all the water that was in the Nile turned to blood" (v. 20). In trying to understand what happened, several facts need to be considered and evaluated. Obviously, not all of the water in Egypt was transformed, for there was still some available for the magicians of Pharaoh to use later (v. 22). Further, the Egyptians were also able to duplicate the act of Moses. Whether it was an actual duplication or some sleight-of-hand trick we do not know, but the indication is that it was an actual duplication. It has been suggested that what happened may have been either the thickening and reddening of the river by massive amounts of red clay silt from Ethiopia or the massive growth of some form of red plankton. Both phenomena were not uncommon occurrences. If this is what happened, then the expression "turned to blood" is a figure of speech. Such figures of speech are common in all language, and certainly they occur in the

Bible. But whatever happened, the end result was clearly something foul and dangerous.

If it was a natural occurrence, this does not eliminate the miracle or wonder; it just transforms its nature. It occurred precisely when God said it would. Even natural events do not occur just because a preacher says they will. The miracle may have been literal blood. It may also have been a miracle in the timing of a natural event. Either way, God showed his power over one of the chief gods of Egypt.

There is a fascinating sidelight to this plague. In all of the ancient Near East, there was a common belief that blood was the source of life. This is also true in the Old Testament, which says, "the life of every creature is the blood of it" (Lev. 17:14). The Egyptians considered the Nile to be the source of life; but when it was turned to blood, the real source of life, it caused death on every hand. The two things that the Egyptians considered to be the source of life had combined to bring death.

But Pharaoh paid no attention to all of this. The expression "he did not lay even this to heart" (v. 23) means that he did not even think about it. In the Old Testament, the heart is the seat of thought and will, not of emotion. He refused to consider either what had happened or what it might mean.

Plague 2: the land overrun by frogs (7:25 to 8:15).—The number in "seven days" is also one of those Hebrew numbers which can be understood as either symbolic or actual. The number seven frequently is used to describe a particularly holy, complete number. This would then mean that when the full time that God had determined had passed, the next plague was begun. On the other hand, the number may be literally referring to a week. Thus the second plague would have occurred a week after the first. This is one of the few specific time references in the plague narratives.

Pharaoh was warned before this plague came. Any nation whose major territory was confined to the narrow floodplains of a large river might be expected to have a problem with frogs. This was true in Egypt. They had a goddess (Hekht) whose responsibility it was to protect the land from frogs. Thus this plague, just like the first, was aimed at one of the members of the Egyptian pantheon. When the God of Israel sent frogs, there was nothing Hekht could do.

The first plague had been sent as a result of the announcement of God and Aaron's holding out the rod, then striking the Nile with it. The second plague came in the same way except that Aaron did not strike anything with the rod.

The Egyptian "magicians did the same by their secret arts" (8:7). The miracle from Moses' viewpoint was very likely that of timing. The frogs came when he said they would, at the command of God. If, on the other hand, there was something supernatural about their coming, this does not give too much difficulty insofar as understanding the acts of the magicians. Any good sleight-of-hand artist could produce frogs in seemingly surprising ways.

The nuisance of the frogs got through to Pharaoh, so he begged of Moses and Aaron, "Entreat the Lord." These were strange words on the lips of the Egyptian leader. He was requesting their prayers. However, we must note that all he wanted was relief. He did promise that if Moses would respond, then he would "let the people go to sacrifice to the Lord" (v. 8). He probably had no intention of granting this; but, being desperate, he promised anything.

Moses' response to Pharaoh is significant. He asked that Pharaoh set the time when the deliverance should come. This possibly affirms the fact that the significance of the event was not so much in what happened as in when it happened. This in no way denies the fact of the miraculous power of God; rather, it focuses upon the fact that God is not only powerful but free to act when he pleases.

We should also note that, from Moses' viewpoint, the purpose of the removal was that Pharaoh should "know" that there was no one like the God of Israel. When Pharaoh's own goddess could not deliver Egypt, the God of Israel could.

An interesting sidelight to this event was the problem of the dead frogs. "The land stank" (v. 14). Whoever wrote this knew something of the stench of frogs decaying under the blazing sun. Even in the imagination, the idea is repulsive. The initial days following the end of the plague were probably as bad as the plague itself.

As the days passed, the frogs were gone and the odor was less severe. Pharaoh forgot his promises. This time we are told that "he hardened his heart" (v. 15). Each of the ways of describing what was happening to Pharaoh are probably all describing the same thing from different perspectives. As God pressured him into decisions, Pharaoh became more and more stubborn. But this was just as God had warned Moses.

Perhaps we should also note that even though the Egyptians could duplicate the coming of the frogs, they were not able to rid the land of them. Magicians can make things seem to appear. They certainly could have made them seem to disappear. But there was no way they could get rid of the stench of the dead frogs.

Plague 3: the stinging gnats (8:16-19).—Before we consider the actual events of this plague, we must try to identify the insects involved. The Hebrew word has been variously translated as "lice" (KJV), "gnats" (RSV), "maggots" *(The New English Bible),* "sand flies" or "fleas" *(American Standard Version* margin), and "mosquitoes" *(Broadman Bible Commentary).* Obviously, we do not know precisely what the word means; but it appears to refer to some sort of small, flying, stinging insect. "Mosquitoes" is probably the best translation.

The events of this plague are significantly different from the first two. There was no warning given to Pharaoh. This plague was brought, however, as were the others, by Aaron's stretching out the rod and striking the "dust of the earth" (v. 16). For the first time, the magicians were unable to duplicate the action of Moses and Aaron. The verb form translated "tried" indicates that they tried over and over again. Their failure demonstrated that Moses and Aaron were doing more than performing magic tricks.

At this point the attitude of the magicians began to change. When they were unsuccessful in duplicating the sign, they reported to Pharaoh, "This is the finger of God" (v. 19). We must beware of reading either too much or too little into this statement. It is obvious from the rest of the story that the Egyptians were in no way making any sort of faith commitment to the God of Israel. On the other hand, they were certainly recognizing that the power behind Moses was greater than the power behind them. This is extremely important, for the magicians' power supposedly came from their gods. Thus there was not merely a major victory for the God of Israel over the gods of Egypt; there was also an open admission on the part of these members of Pharaoh's court that this was true.

Pharaoh was still unimpressed. He remained set in his own stubborn thought patterns. He had earlier refused to heed Moses and Aaron. This time he refused to listen to his own advisers. Such a statement from his own people should have at least been taken seriously. What Pharaoh could not understand, he would not consider. His mind was closed. He refused to admit that the God of his slaves could have any power at all.

Plague 4: swarming flies (8:20-32).—With this plague we begin to recognize that the first nine plagues are presented in three cycles of three, with the tenth plague standing out as more significant than and totally different from any of the others. Although more details in the basic introduction of each plague point up this recurring cycle, the following analysis of their introductions will illustrate it. Plagues 1 (blood), 4 (flies), and 7 (hail) are all introduced by Moses' being sent to meet Pharaoh in the open, early "in the morning" (7:15; 8:20; 9:13). Plagues 2 (frogs), 5 (pestilence on the cattle), and 8 (locusts) are all introduced by Moses' being sent "in to Pharaoh" (8:1; 9:1; 10:1). Plagues 3 (gnats or mosquitoes), 6 (boils), and 9 (darkness) are all introduced without warning by an immediate act of Moses and Aaron (8:16; 9:8; 10:21). With the Hebrews' understanding of the number three as a sacred number, indicating completeness and totality, the three threes would be understood as extremely sacred and complete. The last plague, making ten in all, arrives at another sacred number. This numerical emphasis would be understood as expressing just how complete the action of God was.

In dealing with this plague, we are again faced with the problem of trying to understand what actually happened. The Hebrew word literally means "swarms." It seems apparent that the reference was to swarms of insects, but the nature of the insects was not indicated. It is probable that these were swarms of flies because of the large number of decaying frogs in the land. But they may have been any kind of insect, even the sacred scarab beetle. Egypt always ran the risk of being overwhelmed by insects, and their religion provided for protection from this. Once again the God of Israel was demonstrating his superiority over the Egyptian pantheon.

In advance of the plague, Pharaoh was warned of its coming. But the warning had a difference, for with this plague the Hebrews were exempted. God said, "I will put a division between my people and your people" (v. 23). Not only was God showing his power in bringing the plague when he said it would come; he was also showing his sovereignty in being able to control the locality where it would come.

After the plague had come, Pharaoh called for Moses and Aaron and offered a compromise. "Go, sacrifice to your God within the land" (v. 25). The dynamics of this need to be viewed both from Pharaoh's side and from Moses' side. Pharaoh was beginning to feel the pressure and was seeking some way out. At the same time he wanted to keep his slaves.

From Moses' side, the offer was not even worth considering. Anything less than full obedience to God was too little. Further, Moses realized that what they were called upon to do for God would be offensive to the Egyptians. To follow God, they had to leave their world behind. Moses responded in the end, "We must go" (v. 27).

Pharaoh, grasping at straws and seeking to get Moses to settle for something less, offered a second compromise. He offered to grant part of the demand but not all of it. "I will let you go . . . ; only you shall not go very far." In modern terms, it might be said, "If you must seek to follow God, do not go to church very often and do not get involved in any form of real Bible study or serious service." "Go to church, but do not make a commitment to Christ." Following the offer of the second compromise, Pharaoh made a pious plea again: "Make entreaty [pray] for me" (v. 28).

It was obvious to Moses that if they ever got to the wilderness, there was no way Pharaoh could control how far they went. So he agreed to pray for Pharaoh. But he also recognized the possibility of Pharaoh's treachery and warned him against dealing "falsely" (v. 29). So Moses prayed and God responded by removing the plague. As expected, Pharaoh continued in his stubborn refusal when the plague had been removed.

Plague 5: the pestilence upon the cattle (9:1-7).—All attempts to identify the precise nature of this plague have been unsuccessful. Anthrax has been frequently suggested and would certainly fit the fatal nature of the plague, but there is no real basis for drawing this conclusion. It is sufficient to note its devastating effect without pressing its identity. "Cattle" obviously refers to all domesticated animals.

Pharaoh was again warned that this plague was coming, and a specific time was given for its onset. This was also a direct blow at the Egyptian religious system. All animal life was sacred to the gods of Egypt, and the Apis bull was considered to be divine. This particular god was shown to be impotent in the face of Yahweh, and all other gods were shown to be unable to protect that which belonged to them. The God of Israel was again victorious.

For the second time a distinction was made between the Egyptians and the Hebrews. "The cattle of the Egyptians died, but of the cattle of the people of Israel not one died" (v. 6). This kind of distinction had occurred with the plague of swarming insects. But there was a difference pointed out in relation to the plague upon the cattle. Pharaoh himself checked out the truth of the report and saw for himself that God had the power to make this kind of separation.

All of the plagues up to and including this one had struck at the heart of Egyptian religion—a series of emotional blows. Since they had also made the Egyptians extremely uncomfortable, they were a serious series of physical blows. But this plague struck at the Egyptians' property. The loss of cattle must have been a costly matter. Hitting a person in his bank account almost always gets his attention. But Pharaoh still stubbornly refused to grant Moses' demand.

Plague 6: the boils on man and beast (9:8-12).—This plague, completing the second cycle of three, again came without any warning. The fact that it came upon "man and beast" points up the biblical use of figurative speech. In the preceding plague we were told that *"all* the cattle of the Egyptians died" (9:6). Obviously this was a figure of speech meaning that many or multitudes died. Language has always been used this way, and we should not be surprised when it is so used in the Bible. There were some Egyptian cattle ("beasts") still around to experience this plague.

Moses performed a typical symbolic act of a prophet. In the Old Testament, the prophets regularly carried out actions that were symbolic and that were believed in some way to actually affect historical events (Isa. 20:2-4; Jer. 19:10-11; Ezek. 4:1-3). The ashes or soot which Moses scattered blew over the land. Following this, the people began breaking out in severe "boils" or "skin blisters."

These "boils" would have had two effects. The first was one of pure discomfort. At this point, our author recorded the discomfort of the magicians with a sense of hearty humor. They had earlier been forced to give up their contest with the God of Israel. Now they could no longer even protect their own bodies. But there was a deeper meaning to this plague.

In the ancient Near East, leprosy was the most dreaded disease. It was horrible in its ultimate effect, literally causing the flesh to decay and drop off the living body. There was no way of treating it. The only way of preventing its spread was to isolate the leper. Thus a leper could not enter into a place of worship, visit a market, or be in touch with other people. However, in its earlier stages, leprosy was difficult to diagnose. Therefore anyone with a skin disease had to be isolated until it became clear whether or not he had leprosy.

So when people in Egypt began breaking out with these boils, they would have been treated as if they had leprosy. Such a quarantine of major portions of the populace would have severely disrupted the government, economy, and religion of Egypt. They had a multiplicity of gods, but the plague of boils would have brought the observances at the shrines to a limp if not to a halt. Once again the God of Israel was sovereign, putting the entire system of Egypt to flight.

In spite of all of this pressure from God, Pharaoh still refused Moses' demands. Although it had been said earlier that God would harden Pharaoh's heart (4:21), this is the first time that "the Lord hardened the heart of Pharaoh" (v. 12). Pressure from God either causes a man to turn in repentance or to get more firmly set in his willful way. It had the latter result upon Pharaoh.

Plague 7: the hailstorm (9:13-35).—Beginning the third cycle of three, the events of this plague are perhaps the easiest to understand. There was a massive hailstorm, accompanied by terrifying thunder and lightning. The "fire flashing" (v. 24) obviously refers to lightning.

A number of significant details are recorded about this plague and its meaning. The time of the year is clearly indicated in verses 31–32: "The flax and the barley were ruined, for the barley was in the ear and the flax was in bud. But the wheat and the spelt were not ruined, for they are late in coming up."

This would date the storm in mid-January, the time when these agricultural details were true in Egypt. This also explains why, following such a devastating storm, there was herbage available for the locusts to devour in the next plague. It was the early crops which the storm destroyed, while the later crops had not yet germinated.

The purpose of this plague is clearly stated: "that you may know that there is none like me in all the earth" (v. 14). We must remember that Pharaoh was meant to learn about God through experience. Did he ever!

The expression "upon your heart" (v. 14) is also a new statement. Not merely was the storm going to hit the crops of Egypt; it was going to devastate the heart (or "mind") of Pharaoh. This was probably a reference to the terrifying nature of the storm to come.

Significantly, although God could have destroyed Pharaoh, he had allowed him to live (vv. 15-17). Pharaoh probably did not feel that he had experienced God's mercy, but he had. The providence of God had been aimed at showing Pharaoh that God was merciful in his use of power.

In spite of God's power and mercy, Pharaoh had not learned anything. He was "still exalting" (v. 17) himself. The height of sin is self-exaltation.

God's warning before this plague urged Pharaoh to protect his servants and his cattle. This too was a new dimension to the plagues. Never before had any protection been offered to the Egyptians. In response to this warning, some of the people heeded God and some did not. At least some of the Egyptians were beginning to take God seriously.

When the storm finally came, the Hebrews were again exempted. Although hail was not unusual in Egypt, the ferocity of this storm was unusual. Further, it came when Moses said it would and where he said it would.

When the storm broke, the king of Egypt sent for Moses and Aaron. He said, "I have sinned this time; the Lord is in the right, and I and my people are in the wrong" (v. 27). He further requested that Moses would pray for his deliverance, but only from the storm. There was no indication of repentance on Pharaoh's part—just an admission of guilt. At least, that was a major step. This was also a pretty strong statement for a man who had only recently asked, "Who is the Lord?" (5:2).

Moses recognized Pharaoh's statement for just what it was, but he still gave Pharaoh the chance to prove otherwise. Nothing had changed. Pharaoh returned to his old stubbornness.

This plague was also aimed straight at the heart of Egyptian religion. They had gods who were supposed to protect the crops and ensure a plentiful harvest. Once again, the God of Israel had shown himself more powerful than the gods of Egypt.

Plague 8: the devouring locusts (10:1-20).—The preceding plague of hail had destroyed the earlier crops; but about four to eight weeks later, the wheat and spelt would have been approaching maturity. The plague of locusts obviously came within this period.

A twofold purpose was stated for this and the other plagues. One purpose was that God could "show these signs" (v. 1). We must remember that a sign points to a meaning beyond itself. What God was doing was not just showing his power but proclaiming his absolute sovereignty. Secondly, the plagues were used so that Israel should "know" (experience) (v. 2) the sovereignty of God and bear witness to it in future generations. God's acts are always witnesses to his lordship. When we have observed them and experienced them, we are expected to bear witness to them.

In the light of the overall context, we should note the expression "I have made sport of the Egyptians" (v. 2). It is obvious that God has not just been playing with the Egyptians. This had been a deadly serious contest between the gods of Egypt and the God of Israel. But the pitiful, puny efforts of the Egyptians in behalf of their gods had been a laughing matter. In a very real sense, the contest of the plagues was a historical equivalent of the song of Israel's worship which said, "He who sits in the heavens laughs; the Lord has them in derision" (Ps. 2:4).

Again, Moses and Aaron went to Pharaoh with the divine warning. There was a new dimension to this warning, put in the form of a question. "How long will you refuse to humble yourself before me?" (v. 3). This was quite a demand for a man who was considered by both his people and himself to be divine. The god-king of Egypt was being called upon for submission to the God of his slaves. It would have been a ridiculous demand except for the fact of what had happened in the preceding plagues. The underlying question was whether Pharaoh had learned anything from the first seven plagues. In the Hebrew understanding of numbers, seven was a complete number. From Israel's standpoint, seven plagues should have been enough; but this was not true.

The announcement of the coming of the plague of locusts was also clearly aimed at a god of Egypt. Although locusts were not the problem in Egypt that they were in Canaan, they were still enough of a problem that they had a god who was to protect the crops from their incursions. So this was another deliberate confrontation with Egyptian religion. Following the presentation of this warning, Moses departed.

At this point, a strange incident occurred. We have been watching the reactions of Pharaoh's servants to the series of catastrophes. There was a major development here, for the royal advisers urged Pharaoh to try to make a deal with Moses by letting "the men go." A major rebuke was given to the Egyptian king when they said, "Do you not yet understand that Egypt is ruined?" (v. 7). The economy of the land had been devastated. The leaders could not see how they could stand any more. So Pharaoh called Moses and Aaron back and offered a new compromise.

The narrative here is extremely lively and entertaining. It is rather typical of diplomatic negotiations of any age. A lot was implied which was not said. Also, a lot was said which had a double meaning. At first, Pharaoh seemed to be granting the demand of Moses when he said, "Go, serve the Lord your God." Then he appeared to have an afterthought, for he followed with a question, "But who are to go?" (v. 8). Moses bluntly responded that they were all going and they planned on taking everything they possessed. Pharaoh apparently was hoping that the concession he had made might have tempted Moses to ease his demands a bit. He was surely disappointed.

In a statement dripping with sarcasm, Pharaoh gave a blessing. He hoped that God's guidance would be as nonexistent as the royal permission for which they had been asking. Then he accused them of planning something evil against Egypt. He knew this was not true. If they had had such a purpose, they would have carried it out in the land. In typical diplomatic fashion, he tried to raise a nonexistent issue to avoid facing the real one. Then, with an appearance of great generosity, he offered to allow the men to go to serve the Lord. In the ancient Near East, most worship was carried on by men. As heads of families, they represented the family before their gods. This was true in most of Israel's worship. Pharaoh was implying that all Moses had asked for was the opportunity to worship God. If this were true, then the men could do it. But if this had been granted, they would certainly have returned to Egypt.

Although we are not told how Moses responded to Pharaoh's compromise, the fact that Pharaoh had Moses and Aaron "driven out" (v. 11) from his presence suggests a complete rejection.

The locusts came as an obvious manifestation of natural events. An east wind blew "all that day and all that night," coming in from the wilderness of Sinai. "The east wind had brought the locusts" (v. 13). The miracle was again one of timing rather than of event. It was a devastating plague. In response to the divine catastrophe, Pharaoh again confessed, "I have sinned" (v. 16). But we still must not see this in any way as repentance. Rather, it was regret at the punishment. He again begged Moses to pray to God "to remove this death from me" (v. 17). All Pharaoh cared to do was to escape the plague.

In a manner similar to the way they had come, the locusts were removed. "A very strong west wind . . . lifted the locusts and drove them into the Red Sea" (v. 19).

As usual, when the locusts were gone, Pharaoh was unchanged. God's pressure upon him had only caused him to become more set in his own will and purpose. Therefore "he did not let the children of Israel go" (v. 20).

Plague 9: the oppressive darkness (10:21-29).—This plague brings an appropriate conclusion to the three cycles of three, for it struck at the most important of Egypt's gods, the sun.

As at the end of each of the first two cycles, there was no warning given to Pharaoh. Suddenly the sun was covered, and an intensive, awesome, oppressive darkness enveloped the land. The Bible describes it as "a darkness to be felt" (v. 21). It is also described as "thick darkness." (v. 22). The latter expression is literally a "dark darkness." The use of two different words for darkness really gives emphasis to the blackness.

The question of the real nature of the event may be impossible to solve. Some have suggested an unexpected eclipse of the sun. This can be quickly rejected for two reasons. As accomplished astronomers, the Egyptians were able to predict movements of the heavenly bodies centuries in advance. It is inconceivable that they would have been caught by surprise by an eclipse. Furthermore, no eclipse ever lasts for such a period of time as is described here. Even if the "three days" (v. 23) is a figure of speech, it surely described a longer period than that covered by a solar eclipse.

On the other hand, it has been suggested a massive sandstorm blew in from the desert. Certainly, the major winds described in the preceding plague could have accomplished something like this. The "west wind" that blew away the locusts would have been coming off the great Sahara desert. If it had brought a massive sandstorm, this would have been literally "a darkness to be felt." It is quite possible that the ninth plague could have been this kind of event. Then the miracle would not have been so much in what happened as in the timing and control of the sovereign God.

But it is also possible that this plague could have been some sort of supernatural manifestation by which the sunlight of Egypt was blackened. This would have been extremely terrifying for a people who worshiped the sun. Whatever happened, there was no question in either Moses' or Pharaoh's mind but that Yahweh had done it.

As a further justification of this belief, the "people of Israel had light where they dwelt" (v. 23). Whether it was a sandstorm or some supernatural event, it did not occur in Goshen.

In his terror, Pharaoh called for Moses and offered a fourth compromise: "Go, serve the Lord; your children also may go with you; only let your flocks and your herds remain behind" (v. 24). This may have been the last gasp of Pharaoh. But it was also a very subtle temptation to Moses. They were being given freedom to go with all the people. But Pharaoh knew that if Israel's possessions remained in Egypt, they would not go very far; nor would they stay away.

Moses' response was one last rejection of Pharaoh's compromises. His plea to Pharaoh was that he was ignorant of what God was going to require of them. Pharaoh again refused to give the ultimate permission. He had been driven to the brink of yielding, but he still would not do so. The pressure from God had been building, but it caused the Egyptian king to become even more set in his stubborn ways. In overwhelming anger, he ordered Moses to "get away" (v. 28) from him. In that same outburst of temper, he threatened Moses with death if he ever appeared at the palace again.

Moses responded either in anger or in humor. Unfortunately, there is no way we can recover the tone of voice with which he answered. If he answered in anger, he was saying to Pharaoh that he had been given his last chance. Now there would be nothing left but for the king to experience the full wrath of God. On the other hand, if Moses was responding in humor, he would have been almost laughing, saying to Pharaoh: "You are so right. You will never see me again, for when you next start really looking for me, I'll be gone."

Some have raised the question as to how this episode fits in with that recorded in Exodus 12:31-32, where Moses and Aaron were apparently called before Pharaoh again. It has been suggested that they were just sent a message and did not really appear before Pharaoh. That may be true. On the other hand, the words spoken at the end of the ninth plague were spoken in the heat of anger (at least by Pharaoh). To hold that a man must live up to everything he speaks in anger is to demand more than is justified.

The Night of the Passover (11:1 to 13:22)

The final plague stands out from those that preceded it because it was so different and drastic. The length of the narrative and the events that surrounded it make it stand out. Even more important, it was the event that finally broke Pharaoh's resistance.

The warning issued (11:1-10).—It is obvious that this was to be the last plague: "Afterwards he will let you go." Not only was Pharaoh going to stop refusing to let Israel go; he was going to "drive" (v. 1) them away. That was a massive turnabout.

In addition, the Egyptians were going to be so glad to get rid of Israel that they were going to pay them to leave. The statement that "Moses was very great in the land of Egypt" (v. 3) described his growing reputation among the people. Pharaoh was finally going to accept this as well.

The announcement of this plague arouses horror, but its significance was greater than just suffering. In the ancient religions, the firstborn of man or beast was the particular property of the gods. Egypt had hundreds of gods, but not a single god would be able to protect his particular property.

Further, we should note that the announcement of this plague was a part of Moses' final words to Pharaoh. When this last warning had been made, Moses "went out from Pharaoh in hot anger" (v. 8).

That final warning included a graphic description of the predicted departure from Egypt. To underscore the coming "distinction between the Egyptians and Israel" are two remarkable predictions. First is the statement that "not a dog shall growl" (v. 7) against the Hebrews. The Egyptians were going to be so glad to get rid of Israel that even their dogs would not growl as they went out. Second, Moses told Pharaoh that the royal servants were going to "bow down" (v. 8) in submission before Moses (and his God) and beg them to leave the land. This was quite a contrast to the picture of the arrogant king who had said that he would never let them go.

Verse 10 is a restatement of everything that had gone before. With signs and wonders God had applied his pressure to Pharaoh, but the king had become steadily more stubborn. Now the stage was set for the final scene.

The instructions for the Passover (12:1-13).—The statement of the time is possibly a mistranslation. The Hebrew literally says: "This month is the first of the months for you; it is the first month of the year for you" (writer's translation). This apparently meant that what they had been recognizing as the beginning of their year was becoming the beginning of their real existence. It had been the beginning of the year. It was becoming the beginning of life. The word "month" literally means new moon. The particular month in question was Abib (called Nisan after the exile), the equivalent of our April–May.

It has been suggested that this Passover observance was the festival that Moses wanted to observe in the wilderness, but there is no evidence for this. Surrounding nations did have some sort of spring religious festival. For Israel, however, the Passover was tied precisely to the deliverance from Egypt. God's mighty acts served as the basis for this celebration.

The people were given instructions for selecting a lamb and preparing it. This was in no way similar to the typical sacrifice. The first matter of importance was the daubing of the blood.

For the Hebrews, the blood was the seat of life. (See the discussion on the plague of blood, 7:14-24.) The plague that was about to come upon the land was a visitation of death. By daubing the sides of the doorway with blood, God was saying to them that he had blocked the entrance of death by his gift of life. In a similar way the blood of Jesus bars the access of spiritual death to us.

The entire lamb was to be consumed. What was not eaten was to be burned. By eating the lamb, they became identified with the lamb; he literally became a part of their life. They were to "eat it in haste" (v. 11), as a symbol of the fact that they had to be ready to depart when God opened the way.

Further, it is most important to recognize that the death blow to the Egyptian firstborn was a blow at their gods. Yahweh said, "On all the gods of Egypt I will execute judgments" (v. 12). The blood was a sign of God's protection, of his gift of life.

For the first time, whether anyone experienced the plague was not a question of race but one of faithful obedience. Whoever did not trust and obey would not be spared. In this last plague, deliverance became a matter of faith. Did one believe God enough to obey him?

The feast of unleavened bread (12:14-20).—In connection with the Passover, a second feast was observed, that of unleavened bread. The Passover was a one-night affair; the Feast of Unleavened Bread was a seven-day observance. Behind the prohibition against leaven may have been a belief that leaven was intrinsically evil. It was a symbol for corruption. When Moses finally gave the commands for this festival to the Hebrews, he cited as the reason for the use of unleavened bread the haste with which they had to depart. There obviously was not time to wait for leaven to work through the dough (12:33-34).

Implementation of the Passover (12:21-28).—When Moses gathered the elders to tell them how to observe the Passover, he added several details that had not been given before. He described how to put the blood upon the doorposts and the lintel. The word translated as "basin" was also used to mean the threshold. If this was the meaning here, it would be probable that the lamb was slain at the entrance and his blood poured out upon the threshold. Then it would have been applied to the sides and top. Thus the symbolism would have been that the doorway was completely blocked by the blood.

For protection, no one was to "go out of the door of his house until the morning" (v. 22). "The destroyer" (v. 23) has been variously interpreted. It probably meant nothing more than the angel of death. Certainly the Hebrews did not understand it in any way as demonic, for God had clearly stated that he was going to be the One passing through on the night of death (11:4-5).

They were told that this was to be a perpetual celebration of theirs on the anniversary of their deliverance. Obviously, when such a ritual would be observed in far distant days, the children who would subsequently have been born would have no idea of its meaning or significance. Their questions would be natural and must have an answer. Even now the questions of the children are built into the Passover observance of contemporary Judaism. But the point in Moses' instructions was not so much that the children should ask such questions as a part of the ritual. His point was that children naturally would ask questions about the ritual. Thus the ultimate meaning was that the parents and leaders of Israel were to be responsible for seeing that their children were told what God had done for them.

The elders' response to Moses' message was one of wonder and awe, for they "bowed their heads and worshiped" (v. 27). But there is also a hidden meaning here. They were slaves in Egypt. In spite of Moses' efforts, there had not been any movement toward freedom. Suddenly, with renewed emphasis, they were told that they had a future in God's Promised Land. They were being given rituals to celebrate when they arrived at their destination. Here was a renewal of hope. On the night of darkness and death they were looking forward to light and life with God.

The night of death (12:29-42).—There is no way of recapturing the devastation of Egypt on the night of death. The dark stillness

was suddenly broken by weeping. Forgetting his wrathful pledge that
he would never see Moses and Aaron again, Pharaoh sent for them.
In his grief he urged them to depart. The mighty pharaoh cried out
his final words from the agony of his heart: "Bless me also!" (v. 32).
Not any of the gods of Egypt had been able to protect their firstborn.
Not even the god-king himself had been able to do so.

In their departure, the Hebrews asked the Egyptians for gifts. This
must be understood as neither bribery nor thievery. Slaves about to
face the wilderness needed supplies of food and clothing. They also
needed treasure to buy additional supplies along the way. They would
come across nomads from whom they could make purchases.

So they left Egypt behind. The number of the gathering gives a
problem. "Six hundred thousand men" seems far too large, although
the same figure is given in Numbers 11:21. This would make the
total Hebrew population somewhere about two to three million. That
many people could have walked out of Egypt any time they wished,
for Ramses in his greatest battle had only twenty thousand fighting
men. Among the many proposed solutions, the most likely one focuses
upon the Hebrew word that is translated "thousand." It is also used
in both the Old Testament and in other ancient literatures as either
"clan" or "fighting unit" (perhaps similar to company or platoon).
Thus it could refer to six hundred clans or fighting units. This would
give a total population of about twenty-five thousand and would fit
all the biblical evidence. (For a more detailed consideration, read
The Broadman Bible Commentary, vol. 1, pp. 349–351.)

As they left, they were accompanied by a "mixed multitude" (v.
38). We do not know precisely who these were. They were probably
other slaves, perhaps with Semitic backgrounds. There may also have
been some Egyptian hangers-on who had begun taking Moses seriously. But since they did not really have the faith of Israel, they became
a source of problems all along the way (see Num. 11:4).

The "four hundred and thirty years" (v. 41) that they were said
to have been in Egypt also gives a problem. Ancient use of figures
was frequently more symbolic than literal in meaning. Thus they become difficult to deal with. The Septuagint says that this period covered the time they were "in Egypt and in Canaan," thus including
the entire patriarchal period as well. It is obvious that we have a
textual problem here and that the actual period in Egypt was apparently considerably less. Since we do have problems with the actual

transmission of this text, we can just recognize the difficulty and await further developments in historical, archaeological, and textual studies. (See *The Broadman Bible Commentary,* vol. 1, pp. 351–352.)

The participants in the Passover (12:43-51).—One of the problems in this material dealing with the Passover and the Feast of Unleavened Bread is the way it keeps shifting back and forth from subject to subject. We return here for a few verses on the regulations governing participation in the Passover. It was to be a family celebration. Slaves could observe it after they had been made a part of the covenant community through circumcision. The only strangers who could participate were those whose entire family had become a part of the covenant community. It was the divine intent that only those who had publicly identified themselves with the Israelite family could take part. No exceptions were to be made.

God's purposes (13:1-16).—The last divine words to Moses and through Moses to Israel concerning these events had to do with God's purposes. The firstborn were peculiarly the property of God. They were to be devoted to him. In their belief, it was the firstborn male through whom the heritage of life was considered to be transmitted. The background for this was the death of the firstborn of Egypt. They could not be protected by their gods, but the God of Israel could keep that which was his. The firstborn of the Hebrews was to be kept alive by substituting an appropriate sacrifice. Thus life, not death, was God's gift to his firstborn.

The future celebrations of these events were to serve as memorials to the power of God in delivering the Hebrew people from Egypt. Men have a tendency to forget their history. Religious and national celebrations keep alive such memories. Further, the celebration of Passover was to stir the imagination of the children, so that they would seek to understand what God had done for them. This would give the people an opportunity to retell their divine deliverance.

The concept of binding these words on the wrist and between the eyes was common in the ancient Near East and is referred to in Deuteronomy 6:8 and 11:18. Scripture verses on tiny scrolls were placed in little purses or bags and then tied with thongs around the wrist or around the head. They were later called *phylacteries.* The word translated "mark" literally means sign. Wearing these verses would be an open sign of the identity of the people of God and would remind them of his mighty acts of deliverance.

The departure from Egypt (13:17-22).—As the deliverance from
Egypt had been the result of God's action, so the way selected to
travel from Egypt was the way of God's own leading. Central to the
thought of both Exodus and the Bible was that God was leading.

They were not led out by way of the coastal highway. At that time
in history, the Philistines had not yet settled there. When the event
was recorded in later times, the territory was designated by a name
which had meaning then. At the time of the Exodus event, the coastal
highway was under Egyptian control and was defended by Egyptian
troops. For Israel to be able to leave Egypt in peace, this was certainly
not the route to take.

They were led instead along the caravan routes into the wilderness.
This region was largely unpopulated and would have been lightly
defended, if defended at all. The words translated "Red Sea" literally
mean "Sea of Reeds." We do not know precisely where it was. It
could have been one of several major bodies of water along the border
of Egypt, where now the Suez Canal exists. It had to be large enough
to block the path of Israel and also large enough to overwhelm the
pursuing Egyptian armies. At this point we cannot be more precise.

They went forth prepared to fight ("equipped for battle," v. 18).
But God did not intend for them to fight too soon. They carried the
bones of Joseph with them, as had been promised before he died
(Gen. 50:25). Joseph had never looked upon Egypt as home.

The people departed from Egypt by way of Succoth and Etham.
Although many Bible maps show these places, we do not really know
their precise location. Any identification is tentative and unproven.
All we can say now is that they were between Egypt and the sea,
in the direction of the wilderness.

As they went, God was with them. In the Old Testament, fire is
regularly used as a symbol of God's presence, as we saw at the burning
bush. The column of cloud and smoke was easily identifiable as connected with the fire. Thus both fire and cloud served as constant
reminders of God's presence. The actual event has been variously
explained as some volcanic fire and smoke in the distance that served
to guide them, as a miraculous occurrence right with them, or as
something visionary. Whatever it was, it said to the Hebrews that
God was with them. That was sufficient.

The timing of the plagues.—In the introduction to the commentary
we considered the date of the Exodus event. A second question is

that of the actual time span which the plagues covered. We must understand from the outset that there is no way in which we can be dogmatic about this. On the other hand, some evidence gives us hints by which we can draw conclusions.

First, the last plague is clearly identified as occurring in the month of Abib (13:4), and the Passover was on the fourteenth day of that month (12:6). The month of Abib overlapped the end of March and the first part of April. Thus, the middle of Abib would have been about the end of March.

Second, for the agricultural reasons already mentioned, the plague of hail occurred about mid-January. The plague of locusts that devoured the wheat would have been between four and eight weeks later. This would have been between mid-February and mid-March. It had to be early enough in that period to allow for the plague of darkness to intervene between this and the plague of death.

Third, the only other plague which gives us any possible indication of time is the first one, when the water of the Nile was transformed. If the transformation of the expected life-giving properties of the Nile occurred at the time when the annual flood was expected, as seems likely, this would have been sometime between June and October. Occurring when the snows melted in the highlands of Ethiopia, the more likely time would have been near the beginning of this period.

Thus it would seem that the overall period covered by the plagues would have stretched from June of one year to the end of March in the next. The first plague could have been somewhat later, but could hardly have been any earlier. The period of the plagues would thus have been ten months at the most, and possibly a little bit less.

The plagues accomplished their purpose. Both Israel and Egypt had learned the sovereign power of God. Israel was delivered from the slavery into which it had drifted, but only by the redemptive act of God. As free men, they no longer had to depend upon a faith which had been passed on by their fathers; they had been given a historical experience with the living God. It was to this experience that they always looked back. It was to this experience that the prophets called them back when they strayed away in the future.

Crises That Cripple Faith
14:1 to 18:27

The night of death should have marked the end of Egypt's dealings with Israel. It did not. In one sense, it was the ultimate event of God's deliverance of Israel from slavery; but it was not the end. The final, climactic deliverance took place at the sea. But in the most typical of human reactions, Israel constantly forgot the oppressions of Egypt, only remembering the security it had given.

When Israel began their march out of Egypt, they were filled with hope. It was not long before their hope was replaced by despair. Between the night of the final plague and the day they arrived at Sinai, they were faced by a series of crises that crippled their faith and undermined their hope.

The Divine Purpose Reaffirmed (14:1-4)

Not only had Israel first been led away from the coastal highway (the "way of . . . the Philistines" in 13:17); they were next told to "turn back" from the natural caravan route into the Sinai Peninsula. God was apparently planning to lead them along a less used path to Sinai. The geographical references would have been meaningful to the people of Israel, but they are generally lost to us. We do not know which sea was intended. Pi-ha-hi'roth is a typical Egyptian name referring to a place of meadows, obviously a town in a grassy region, presumably somewhere near Goshen. Migdol means watchtower and probably referred to some border fortress. Several towns with such names are known. Ba'al-zephon means "Baal of the north," obviously a reference to a town dedicated to the Canaanite god Baal.

The reason for this change in direction was given as an enticement to Pharaoh. Their apparent wandering as they went forth would have made the king of Egypt believe that they were lost ("entangled") in the wilderness. The apparent helplessness and hopelessness of Israel would serve to make God's final victory even more magnificent.

Obviously, Pharaoh's scouts were keeping up with Israel's progress. The report of their wanderings must have been relayed to him regularly. No king could afford to have large groups of people wandering around in or near his land without his being constantly aware of it. The temptation brought by Israel's nearness and helplessness and the squeezing pressure from God were going to be too much for Pharaoh. Pharaoh was going to pursue them in order to bring them back. He had never learned that his real adversary was Yahweh, not Israel. Israel was weak. God was not.

The purpose of the whole affair was that God should be glorified by his mighty act and that, once and for all, Israel should experience the sovereign, redemptive power of God. Every act in this divine drama of redemption had been for the purpose of serving as a witness to God. The end result intended was that everyone involved should experience God. Revealing the redemptive nature of God was the ultimate purpose. Men were to learn who God was by what he did.

God's Great Victory (14:5 to 15:21)

Just as God had declared, the temptation to Pharaoh was too great for him to resist. He had forgotten the past already. He decided to go and bring Israel back.

Pharaoh's pursuit (14:5-9).—The expression "when the king of Egypt was told that the people had fled" (v. 5) can be misleading. Pharaoh had not only given Israel permission to go; he had ordered them to go. But as the reports of their progress, or lack of it, were brought back, he became aware that they had really left. They were gone for good. Their departure had done away with a major source of cheap labor. As the economic consequences of their flight began to sink home, both Pharaoh and his people regretted their action in releasing the Hebrews from slavery.

Recognizing the opportunity he thought he had been given by the apparent aimless wandering of Israel, Pharaoh decided to pursue them. His intent was not to fight them, as he would have done with an invading army. His intent was to recapture them. This was more of a police action seeking escaped prisoners than a military action facing an opposing army. He made ready his own chariot and took his people with him. The word translated "army" literally means people. He did not take a slow-moving army with him. They would not have been effective in rounding up fleeing slaves. He took fast-moving chariotry that could overtake and round up the slaves on the edge of the wilderness.

We can easily be misled by the statement that he "took six hundred

picked chariots and all the other chariots of Egypt" (v. 6). The word
"other" is not present in the Hebrew. Further, the statement can
be translated: "He took six hundred picked chariots, even all the chariots (of that kind) of Egypt." The idea seems to have been that he
took his choicest detachment of chariotry, those best suited for the
desert pursuit he anticipated. Thus they could have moved fast with
few problems of supply. To have moved a major army would have
required more planning and less speed. The "officers" who were "over
all of them" also seems to be a mistranslation of the Hebrew. The
word literally means "thirds." Apparently this was a reference to the
chosen crews who manned the chosen chariots. When Pharaoh set
out, he had his choicest chariots with his best crews. He intended
for nothing to slow him down.

So he set forth with this picked force to overtake "the people of
Israel as they went forth defiantly" (v. 8). Literally, they "went forth
with a high hand." Although this may refer to the attitude of the
Hebrews, it also may refer to the fact that God's mighty act had
been done with "a high hand." This seems the preferable interpretation. Israel was not so much going out in defiance as they were going
out through the deliverance of God's sovereign power.

Those who pursued Israel were Pharaoh's chariotry, his people,
and his "horsemen." At this time in history, the Egyptian armies did
not use cavalry as a major portion of their army. Instead, the horsemen
would have served as detachments of scouts, locating and keeping
up with the Hebrews as the rest of the Egyptians drew near.

Although Israel had been gone for some number of days, their slow-
ness and their frequent changes of direction had prevented them
from getting out of Egyptian territory. Pharaoh made haste and over-
took them where they were encamped by Pi-ha-hi'roth. It is obvious,
then, that the events of verses 5-9 had been transpiring while Israel
had been on the march. The Egyptians and the Hebrews had both
been on the move at the same time. For the purpose of recording
these events, they had to be written one after the other.

At this point, the scene was set for the last confrontation. Pharaoh
thought that he was still confronting Israel. He had not yet realized
that he was confronting Israel's God. This failure was to be his
downfall.

Faith's frightened failure (14:10-18).—In the face of the crisis of
Pharaoh's pursuit, the faith of the Hebrews collapsed. Panic gripped

their minds and hearts. "They . . . cried out to the Lord" (v. 10). This was not so much a prayer for deliverance as a cry of blame. As is typical, they quickly turned from crying to God to crying to Moses. It is so easy to see ourselves in the actions of Israel. When everything was going all right, Moses was a great man. As soon as trouble came, they wished that he had left them alone. There may have been a pun intended in their statement that there were "no graves in Egypt" (v. 11). Few nations in the history of the world seem to have been as concerned with tombs, death, and funeral practices as was Egypt. On the other hand, the pun may have been accidental. The situation was probably too serious for that kind of levity. They were saying that it would have been better to have died of old age in Egypt than to be killed in the wilderness before the might of Pharaoh.

In their further questions, their whole implication was that they had never had any desire to be free from the slavery in Egypt. There is no record that they had ever said to Moses: "Let us alone and let us serve the Egyptians." But when they faced the new crisis, this was certainly what they wished they had said. With Pharaoh's army drawing near, they totally caved in. It never dawned on them that Pharaoh had not come out to kill but to recapture them.

The collapsing faith of the Hebrews makes Moses' great statement of faith all the more emphatic. In the face of their terror, Moses cried out to them, "Fear not, stand firm, and see the salvation of the Lord" (v. 13). The "salvation" of which Moses spoke was used in the sense of military victory. The biblical concept of salvation moves forward from this early meaning to the latter one of spiritual deliverance from sin and death. Moses confidently predicted that God was going to win a mighty victory over Pharaoh and that after this, Egypt would no longer be a problem to Israel. His faith was based upon his past experience with God and upon God's recent revelation.

On the other hand, we can also see the implication that Moses found it easier to proclaim his faith than to practice it. We have the same problem. There is no record of what Moses said to God after he had proclaimed his faith to Israel. But God's response "Why do you cry to me?" implies that Moses privately had been wanting to know what God was going to do. Apparently, he thought that God was allowing the Egyptians to draw a bit too close for comfort.

God's message to Moses was startling. "Tell the people of Israel to go forward" (v. 15). "Forward" was into the sea. At first glance that seemed impossible. But God told Moses to raise his rod and "divide" the sea. That literally means to split or cleave it. The image is that of cutting a channel through something hard. What a miracle that was going to be!

The promise to Moses was twofold. Israel should cross the sea. Not even a major body of water could stand before the power of God in leading them to the land of his promise. However, after Israel crossed, Egypt would follow; and in the process God would receive "glory" from the event. The word for "glory" means to be made heavy or to become significant. The mighty act of God would make him significant over all of the gods whom Egypt served and who were expected to grant victory to the arms of Egypt. Further, as a result of this mighty act, the Egyptians were to have fully experienced the sovereignty of Yahweh, the God of Israel.

The victory at the sea (14:19-29).—When the Egyptian force drew near, to all apparent purposes they had the Hebrews pinned against the sea. It would have appeared obvious to any observer that Israel's situation was hopeless. But such a conclusion would have failed to consider God. The "angel of God" in the form of the pillar of cloud moved between the two peoples. As noted earlier (3:2), this expression refers in some sense to an extension of God's own personality, just as the pillar of cloud did. The presence of the cloud served to keep the two peoples separate. When Israel needed guidance, God gave it. When they needed protection, he gave that also. From Egypt's standpoint, the heavy cloud served only to delay their certain victory. From Israel's standpoint, it served to give Moses time to obey God and to allow for the separation of the waters.

"Moses stretched out his hand and the Lord drove the sea back by a strong east wind all night." God could have done the latter whether or not Moses had held out his hand at the beginning. The point behind Moses' outstretched hand was to let Israel know that this was no freak of nature but the direct act of God. We need to note again that the nature of this miracle was not the wind (which was perfectly normal), but a wind of sufficient force which occurred at the right place and at the right time.

The expression "made the sea dry land" (v. 21) is an obvious figure of speech. The sandy bottom was dry enough for Israel to cross on foot, but was soft enough that the wheels of the Egyptians' chariots bogged down when they tried the same thing.

On the other side of the sea, the Hebrews had finally finished cross-ing. Moses was again commanded to stretch out his hand. The wind of God apparently stopped blowing, and the sea waters rushed back into the void and swept over that part of the Egyptian forces which had driven into the sea bottom and become stuck there. The God of Israel had defeated the gods of Egypt. The Egyptians had expected their gods to guarantee victory. Instead, they had suffered a humiliating defeat.

The victory celebration (14:30 to 15:21).—As the end of Egyptian bondage came, the awesome nature of the catastrophic victory dawned upon the Hebrews. The tumult of the returning waters ceased. The writer recorded an eyewitness detail that grips the imagination. "Israel saw the Egyptians dead upon the seashore" (v. 30). Their first reaction was obviously one of awe. Not only did Israel see the dead Egyptians; they realized the nature of the event that had brought this to pass. They "saw the great work which the Lord did." The deepest consequences of this experience were seen in three outward expressions of their inner emotions. They stood in holy terror before the mighty power of their God. He had done what he had promised. Growing out of this was a faith in his redemptive power, for "they believed in the Lord" (v. 31). As a part of their faith in God, a new trust was placed in the man whom God had sent.

Slowly, as the shock of the experience began to wear off, the awe and terror were replaced by an overwhelming joy. They were free at last. Their gratitude at the mighty act of God led them to burst forth into song. Any attempt to analyze the great victory song (vv. 1*b*-18) as to who said what and any attempt to try to determine how long after the actual event it was sung is an exercise in futility. Obviously, such magnificent poetry did not just spring forth extemporaneously. On the other hand, such an overwhelming victory produced great emotions; and great emotions produce great poetry. Further, as we read the introductory words (vv. 19-20) to the song of Miriam (v. 21), there is an impression that this was the first song to be sung. It may have served as the impetus for the other.

Whatever their order, the song of Miriam, accompanied by dancing, led the people in an exuberant celebration "to the Lord, for he has triumphed gloriously" (v. 21). More stately but no less joyous was the song of Moses. Beginning with the same words as the song of Miriam, it proceeds with a theological statement of God's nature (vv.

2-3), continues through a recounting of the great deliverance (vv. 4-10), restates God's unique nature (vv. 11-12), moves to a statement of God's future great acts (vv. 13-17), and concludes with a final affirmation of faith (v. 18).

Three major ideas stand out in this majestic hymn of victory. First, there was the realization and affirmation that the deliverance over Pharaoh was the result of God's act. He may have used the wind to accomplish it, but it was God who did it. When Israel looked at the events of the sea, they did not seek to explain the event away by appeals to all the secondary causes; they simply saw God at work.

Second, there was a magnificent hope for the future. Based upon God's acts in the past, they placed their faith in him to complete his purposes to bring them in and plant them in the place which he had promised them. We must recognize that their faith and confidence would not always be so strong. But at the moment of God's victory, they could look forward confidently to future victories.

Third, the most profound set of ideas in this hymn are those concerned with the nature of God (vv. 2-3,11-12,18). The hymn states with boldness that God was the source of "strength," "song," and "salvation." "Salvation" in this context obviously referred to a military and physical deliverance. But the Bible soon enlarged this idea to include spiritual deliverance as well. Further, the hymn lays claim to the faith that the God of their heritage ("my father's God") had become real to them ("my God," v. 2). Men do not come to believe in God through argument but through historical experiences. We must meet him to believe in him. One dimension of their faith in God which we sometimes miss was that he was "a man of war" (v. 3). In those ancient times they saw God's visible power in the conquest of his enemies. It was not until later that they realized that the greatest enemy was sin and that the greatest power was love.

"Who is like thee, O Lord, among the gods?" (v. 11). This statement stands as a warning to us not to read all of our New Testament faith back into the Old Testament. At this point in Israel's pilgrimage of faith, they did not yet believe in monotheism (one God only) but in monolatry (only one God for them). All the ancient peoples worshiped many gods. Israel had not yet followed far enough in their faith experience to cast away any concept of other gods. It was a major step forward to believe that God was different from all the others and that he was the only one for them.

The most profound statement of faith in this hymn is the concluding verse. "The Lord will reign for ever and ever" (v. 18). The use of the term "reign" clearly indicated a recognition of the fact that Yahweh was king. Egypt had Pharaoh. Israel had Yahweh. Further, this acknowledgment of his kingship carried with it an implicit submission to his kingly authority. This glorious shout of faith and confidence was to serve as the foundation of Israel's highest faith throughout her history. It was also picked up and enlarged by the author of Revelation, in his triumphant cry: "The kingdom of the world has become the kingdom of our Lord and of his Christ, and he shall reign for ever and ever" (Rev. 11:15). The song of victory has become the foundation of confident faith.

Problems in the Wilderness (15:22 to 18:27)

With such a triumphant conclusion to the slavery in Egypt, Israel marched forth into the wilderness. With the echoes of their song of faith ringing in their hearts, they faced the barren Sinai Peninsula. Following the experience of deliverance from Egypt, they would surely never find their faith lacking or their confidence growing weak. But they did. The crises came quickly, and Israel's faith caved in.

Because the events of the wilderness occurred between the mighty acts of God in the deliverance from Egypt and the mighty power of God in the covenant at Sinai, they are frequently considered to be relatively insignificant. They were of major significance to Israel and should be to us. The two spiritual mountaintops on either side focus on God's gifts. This spiritual valley directed attention to Israel's weak faith. To Israel's faith, the crises were crippling.

Water that proved unusable (15:22-27).—There is no way to trace with any accuracy the exact route which Israel followed into the wilderness. There are some suggested locations of the wilderness of Shur and the oases of Marah and of Elim. The route likely lay somewhere along the western edge of the Sinai Peninsula.

Israel was traveling with flocks and herds, as well as with children. A "three days'" journey would probably have been between thirty and forty-five miles. There may be some significance to the fact that Moses had originally said that they wanted to go a three days' journey to serve God. In actual fact, when they had covered this distance they turned against him. Such is the way of human faith.

The word "Marah" means bitter and was descriptive of the water there. Desert oases were frequently named for the springs or wells that were there, for the water was their central feature. Looking for abundant supplies of fresh water, Israel immediately turned against Moses. It is surely implicit that they also turned against the God who had given Moses to them. Moses took his difficulties to God, and God "showed him a tree" which was able to make the bitter waters sweet. It is possible that Moses, having spent a large portion of his life shepherding the flock of Jethro in similar situations, was familiar with a variety of tree that had such qualities. Modern Arabs say there are such trees. Thus, if this is the case, the significant event here would be that God caused Moses to find the necessary tree. On the other hand, it is just as possible that here was some form of supernatural event. Either way, Moses and Israel were both sure that God had delivered them.

This had been an opportunity for proving or testing Israel. Their grumbling response was a clear indication of just how badly they had failed the test. The divine response to this experience was "a statute and an ordinance" (v. 25) commanding Israel to trust and obey. This is a clear indication that not all of Israel's laws are to be identified with the Sinai experience. Their entire history with God is a history of God's gifts of laws to them. The message here was obviously that if Israel would remain loyal and faithful to God, they would not suffer the plagues that Egypt suffered. Furthermore (and most important), they would discover that God was their "healer" (v. 26). When difficulties came, they would find health from God.

God had dealt gently with them in this first crisis in the wilderness. They had failed their test, but they had also been mercifully delivered. The "twelve springs of water and seventy palm trees" (v. 27) at Elim may be strictly literal. But since both numbers implied completeness or perfection to the Hebrews, they may simply be references to the fact that following God's deliverance, they found an abundant supply of life's necessities.

Hunger that cramped the soul (16:1-36).—After a refreshing rest at Elim, the people set forth again and came into the wilderness of Sin. This is probably in some way connected with Sinai, but its location is unknown. Since they had departed from Egypt on the morning of the fifteenth day of Abib, they would have arrived here exactly a month later. This kind of chronological detail would appear to be based upon an eyewitness account. Following their deliverance from

Egypt and the experience at Marah, it would have seemed that Israel should have learned her lesson. But that was not true.

Food was scarce. The people had quickly forgotten the servitude of Egypt. All they could remember was the "fleshpots" in which meat was cooked. Slaves would probably not have had much meat to eat. But the memory of it seemed sweet. They remembered eating "bread to the full." In the Old Testament, "bread" frequently was used as a figure of speech to refer to any and all kinds of food. It appears to have this meaning here. They remembered having all that they wanted to eat. The hunger of their stomachs made them grumble bitterly against Moses and Aaron. Again we see the frailty of human nature. They had been all too eager for freedom when it cost nothing. Now that it began to make demands upon them, it appeared to be too expensive.

It may seem hard to believe that the same people who had sung the song of victory (15:1*b*-18) could now believe that God had brought them into the wilderness "to kill this whole assembly with hunger" (v. 3). It would be hard to believe *if* we did not recognize the same tendencies in ourselves.

In response to their grumbling, God again dealt with merciful patience. He promised them "bread from heaven." The main emphasis here was upon manna, although there was also reference to the supplying of quail. In this chapter, some of the references to "bread" seem to be specifically confined to the manna and some seem to include the quail as well. The statement "that I may prove them" (v. 4) referred to a testing which was a major purpose behind God's providential care. God was certainly meeting their need. This was an obvious purpose. But they were also being tested to see if, with their weak faith, they could trust God for their daily needs. Moses made it very plain to the people that though they had murmured against Moses and Aaron, their actual complaint was directed "against the Lord."

He further made it plain that the provisions that were about to be made were coming as the direct result of the fact that the Lord had heard (v. 8) their murmurings. God always hears, even when we do not know it. In the answer of God, the people became aware again of the "glory of the Lord" (v. 10). They had forgotten God was with them. The glory pointed up his redemptive presence.

The actual nature of the gifts of quail and manna is uncertain. It is quite possible that these may be natural events that became supernatural because they came when and where God said they would. They may also be supernatural in the full sense of that word. The quail of Sinai are migratory birds that fly north and south over major areas, arriving completely exhausted. Under such conditions they are easy prey for those who hunt them. If this is what happened here, then the miracle would be that they came in response to God's promise. The manna has been understood to be a sweet secretion from desert trees. It drops upon the ground and turns white. Both of these phenomena occur in late spring and early summer, the actual time recorded here.

However you understand the event, for Moses and for Israel it was obviously understood as coming from God. It would seem that such miraculous provision would have led to an open and obedient response of the part of Israel. But they continued to disobey. When in their greed they tried to keep too much, it spoiled (v. 20). On the other hand, when they failed to make provision for the sabbath, they found none at all.

The reference to the sabbath here is the first reference in the Old Testament of what was to become one of Israel's major religious observances. The idea had been reflected earlier (Gen. 2:2-3), although there was no specific reference to it. It is possible that it had been observed earlier and had been lost during the slavery in Egypt. The working times of slaves was not a matter open to their own decision. Whether or not the sabbath had been observed earlier, it would be observed after this. At Sinai, it became one of the major foundation stones of Israel's faith.

In commemoration of God's gracious providence, Israel was to fill a jar with the manna and keep it in the center of their sanctuary. The purpose was obviously that they should never forget God's providential care. Such a remembrance should have served to strengthen weak faith. Again there was a mundane detail given which shows the human nature of the author: "An omer is the tenth part of an ephah" (v. 36). In our terms, an omer is about two quarts, dry measure.

Thirst that dried the spirit (17:1-7).—The people continued to move on their journey "by stages" (v. 1). This is apparently a reference to an orderly journey from one resting place to another. When they reached Rephidim, they seemingly made a major encampment for rest and refreshment. Water was expected, but they did not find it.

Again they lost their faith and turned on Moses and on God. There are at least three different records of the people thirsting and turning on Moses (Ex. 15:22-27; 17:1-7; Num. 20:1-13). It has been suggested that these may be duplicate accounts of the same event. Such an interpretation, although possible, is totally unnecessary. In a wilderness region some oases dry up with changes in climate. There is no reason not to think this was not a separate event. The details are totally different from the earlier experience at Marah.

The expression "found fault with" (v. 2) is a typical legal expression. Apparently, their murmuring this time led to some sort of legal action against Moses. Furthermore, the statement of Moses, "They are almost ready to stone me" (v. 4), underscores this conclusion. The last step in the legal rejection of a leader was stoning (see 1 Sam. 30:6; John 10:31).

Moses condemned his people for putting "the Lord to the proof" (v. 2). It is man who is tried by God, not the reverse. The implication behind Moses' words was that they had put God on trial. How quickly they forgot God's acts of deliverance. But we do the same. When a new crisis comes it is so easy to forget God's past victories.

Moses was commanded to demonstrate God's power before the elders (v. 5). It was to be their responsibility to pass on the word of God's new provision.

A double name was given to this particular place: Massah, meaning proof or test, and Meribah, meaning contention. Thus Israel's geographic memories served as a reminder of their foolish lack of faith. If we did not know human nature so well, we should surely conclude that Israel would never question God again. And their faith was growing through God's gracious care. But they still had their human natures.

Enemies who blocked the path (17:8-16).—Suddenly a crisis of a different kind confronted Israel. The earlier crises that had crippled Israel's faith had been pursuit by an enemy whom they thought had been defeated and the lack of provision in the wilderness when they thought they could not survive. With the Amalekites, there was an enemy in front of them, prohibiting them from continuing on their way to Sinai. The Amalekites were descendants of Esau (Gen. 36:12) and thus related to Israel. They are constantly seen in the Old Testament as Israel's enemies. Although we are not given any reason for their attack here, it was probably based upon the belief that the water and sparse grass of the wilderness was not sufficient for both the Israelites and the Amalekites.

Joshua appears here for the first time. He is obviously Israel's military leader. At this point there was no apparent knowledge that he was one day to succeed Moses in leading Israel. The action of Moses in overseeing the battle is probably best understood in the form of the symbolic actions of the prophets. By such actions they seem actually to have been involved in the release of divine power. This kind of act was always considered to be an outpouring of divine grace. Aaron and Hur are portrayed as faithful servants who literally undergirded their leader in his faithful service. By their aid, with Joshua's military leadership, and as a result of God's power, Israel had the victory.

There is a major new dimension in the conclusion of this episode. Moses was commanded to commit something to writing. The Hebrew has a definite article, making the order refer to "the book." This was apparently a record of the past that was intended to be used as a basis for future actions. It may have been some sort of official journal. This might be considered strange for a leader of slaves. It should not be considered strange for a man who had been trained as a child of Pharaoh. In that capacity, he would have been made knowledgeable of the importance of good records.

The last phrases of this passage have some very difficult Hebrew. Although we cannot be sure of all the details of this passage, it obviously served as a prediction of a long series of future conflicts between Israel and Amalek. The basic meaning seems to have been that God would always serve as an ensign of the armies of Israel.

Troubles that cried for solution (18:1-27).—Following the victory over the Amalekites, Jethro showed up with Moses' family. He apparently came both to see for himself what he had heard about God's mighty deliverances and to reunite Moses with his family. Although we must remember that Jethro was a priest who was descended from Abraham and therefore would have a particular interest in the actions of Yahweh, we should also note that the reports of God's great acts were spreading abroad.

We do not know when or why Moses had sent his wife and family away. It is usually suggested that he had sent them back from Egypt when he began his major conflict with Pharaoh so that they would be protected. We should also note that the Hebrew expression "sent her away" (v. 2) is the one normally used for divorce. It is possible that this may reflect marital problems. If this is true, it might explain why Moses seems to have greeted his father-in-law with more warmth than he did his wife (18:6-7).

When Moses told Jethro "all that the Lord had done" (v. 8), Jethro rejoiced in a cry˙ of praise to God. In addition, he uttered a strong profession of faith when he said, "Now I know that the Lord is greater than all gods" (v. 11). Such a statement would have indicated that his earlier faith had been based upon ancient reports, while he now could point to contemporary experience as a basis for faith. Then Jethro led in a service of sacrifice and a communion meal. In such a celebration, held "before God" (v. 12), it was assumed that God was also a partner to the meal.

On the following day Jethro observed Moses dispensing justice. In the ancient world men came to inquire from God's leader for rulings on all sorts of things from legal cases to matters of faith. It was believed that God spoke through such leaders. Moses was obviously bogged down with such tasks, and they were keeping him from furnishing the leadership that Israel needed. Jethro confronted Moses by boldly stating, "What you are doing is not good" (v. 17). The priest of Midian gave Moses a major lesson in effective leadership and administration.

He called Moses to face his major tasks and get his priorities right. His first task was to be an intercessor, to "represent the people before God" (v. 19). As we shall see later, Moses apparently learned this lesson well. He became one of the Bible's greatest intercessors. Then he called upon Moses to be a teacher to Israel, telling them the words of God. Further, Moses was to be a leader, guiding them in being God's people. Finally, Jethro urged Moses to set up an organization with competent, honest, godly leaders over small groups of the Hebrews. It would be their task to hear the complaints and to dispense justice. Having stated his advice, Jethro urged Moses to implement this if "God so commands you" (v. 23). It was important to Jethro that this advice be followed only if God was in it. Moses found the advice to be good and did as his father-in-law suggested.

Following Moses' organization of Israel for the administration of justice, Jethro returned home. It may appear that his crisis of leadership was of far less significance than the crises of faith and obedience that confronted Israel. Perhaps that is true. Yet Moses' leadership was being seriously weakened by poor organization and administration. These troubles could have as effectively checked the Hebrews' advance to Sinai as any of the others. Leadership problems must be solved just as correctly and effectively as faith problems if God's people are going to accomplish his will on earth.

Every crisis that came to Israel following the night of the Passover was one that could have destroyed them. It was by the patient, gracious leadership of God that they had progressed to Rephidim. From there they were at last ready to move to Sinai.

Surrender That Calls for Cleansing
19:1-25

We have now reached the major turning point in the Exodus experience and in the book itself. The mighty acts of redemption had been completed, and the divine gift of the covenant was about to be made. In the deliverance from Egypt, the complete sovereignty of Yahweh had been demonstrated. He had overwhelmingly shown his absolute control over nature, over Egypt, and over the Egyptian gods. Beginning here and continuing through Leviticus and into Numbers 10, Israel was told by God what his redemption really meant. They were given the covenant as well as a multiplicity of related laws. The covenant and the covenant laws set forth what God was expecting from them. There are some occasional brief narratives along the way, but the basic emphasis is the claim of God upon their lives.

This particular chapter sets forth the preparation demanded of them before the giving of the covenant. It involved three basic emphases: (1) God's invitation to and their acceptance of the covenant life; (2) their consecration in anticipation of the meeting with God; and (3) their realization of the terrifying holiness of God.

Commission and Response (19:1-9a)

As is common in the Old Testament, the initial verse serves as a title for the entire chapter. "The third new moon" after their departure serves to again root the entire episode in history. The Hebrews had left Egypt on the fifteenth day after a new moon. The third new moon following that would indicate that the entire journey had taken about two and one-half months. (For the location of "the wilderness of Sinai," see the commentary material on 3:1-3.) A "wilderness" was not a forest or even a desert, but generally referred to an uninhabited region. It was usually rough, rocky, and uninviting. It was the kind of place where there would be no distractions.

The arrival of the people of Israel and their subsequent encampment at the foot of Sinai must have particularly stirred Moses. The sign which had been given Moses in his initial call had been that Israel would eventually serve God "upon this mountain" (3:12). It would certainly have been with overwhelming awe that Moses would have drawn near this mountain, where it had all begun for him.

Moses was first instructed to remind Israel of the fact that their deliverance, both from Egypt and the wilderness, had been accomplished by God's acts. Following this, he was to set forth the demand for faithfulness: "obey my voice and keep my covenant" (v. 5). God's redemption was accompanied by demands. We must note that obedience did not bring deliverance, but deliverance was expected to be followed by obedience. Israel was told that the end result of such obedience would be a special relationship with God. They would be "a kingdom of priests and a holy nation" (v. 6). This new relation would demonstrate to the world their dedication to God. They were to bear the responsibility of serving as priests (mediators) between the world and God. It is significant that the New Testament picked up this image to describe the nature and function of the Christian community (1 Pet. 2:5,9).

Israel's response to the message of God through Moses was an immediate surrender: "All that the Lord has spoken we will do" (v. 8). It is important to note that they promised obedience without knowing all of the demands of the covenant. They were signing a spiritual blank check.

It is impossible to recapture at this point all of the details of the conversation between God, Moses, and Israel. God certainly did not need Moses to tell him what the people of Israel had said. On the other hand, since he was reporting God's demands to them, it was to be expected (from Israel's standpoint) that he should report their response to God.

Further, God's promise to speak with Moses from the "thick cloud" (v. 9) was intended to demonstrate to Israel that Moses was really

receiving a revelation from God. The thick cloud was a common symbol in the Old Testament for the presence of God. The visible manifestation of God's presence was intended to serve as Moses' authorization
to speak for God.

Consecration and Preparation (19:9*b*-15)

There was obviously more to the conversation between Moses, God,
and Israel than is recorded. Between verse 9*a* and 9*b* there was some
kind of conversation which had to be reported "to the Lord." Since
they were willing to receive God's word and to obey it, the next
step for Israel was to get ready to receive the covenant demands.

The consecration of the people involved several things. The concept
itself rested upon the Old Testament understanding of holiness. The
verb "to consecrate" is the root from which the noun *holy* comes.
Holy basically meant something that was set apart from the world
to God. Places, objects, or people were made holy (or consecrated)
as they were withdrawn from the world and turned over to God.
Viewed from the other direction, such things were made holy as God
took them over and possessed them.

The three days of preparation probably indicated a sacred and complete time for the accomplishment of the necessary cleansing. Although the full ritual of cleansing had not yet been given to Israel,
such rituals were common in the ancient Near East. Israel would
have certainly had some sort of standard procedures through which
they would have gone to accomplish this. The specific commands
given to Israel involved three matters.

They were to wash their garments. This would not have been easy
in the wilderness. But the difficulty did not remove the necessity.
The physical cleansing was probably understood as symbolic of a more
thorough inner cleansing.

In addition, they were to set bounds around the mountain. The
meaning behind this act was that man could not approach God too
closely. The harshness of the penalty for violating this restriction shows
how seriously they were to take it.

The final demand for purification was that they should "not go
near a woman" (v. 15). This expression refers to the sexual relationship.
We must not understand this as indicating a belief that sex was something unclean. The Old Testament has a far higher view of sex than
this. The restriction was aimed at focusing one's energies and attention

on a spiritual confrontation with God. At such a time, nothing was to be allowed to take their attention away from this basic purpose.

The entire ritual of consecration had one essential function: to demonstrate that the approach to God must be taken seriously. The rituals of consecration made sure that anyone approaching God did so with a thorough consciousness of God's awesome holiness.

God's Descent to the People (19:16-25)

When all was ready, the great theophany occurred. The images of thunder, lightning, cloud, fire, and earthquake are familiar ones in the Old Testament for God's drawing near to man. The whole event was an experience of terror for the Hebrews. The sound of the trumpet may have been a part of the divine appearance, or it may have been blown by Moses or Aaron as a part of their response to God. In the ancient world, the trumpet was used for three purposes. It served as a call to worship, as a warning, or as an announcement of the presence of royalty. All three purposes are probably to be understood in the experience as recorded here.

Moses went up to meet with God as God descended to meet with Moses. It is important to note that Moses could approach God only when and as God chose. It is useless to point out that they had already been speaking together. This particular confrontation was of a different kind. This was to be the time of the divine gift of the covenant. As such, this particular conversation was unique. It was, in a sense, God's self-giving. Moses was particularly warned to make sure that the people did not "break through" (v. 21) the boundaries which had been established. The problem was apparently that of controlling the pressures of the curious crowd.

Moses' warning to make special consecration for the "priests" confront us with a strange problem. There is no indication that Israel had priests prior to the giving of the law code at Sinai. It appears that the clan or family leaders served the functions of the priests until the establishment of a regular order of priests. It is probable that the term used here referred to those who fulfilled priestly functions rather than to priests as such.

Having responded to God's invitation by a willing submission, and having made preparation in accord with the divine design, Israel was ready for the awesome approach of God. This is the essential message of the Sinai experience. It is also the message of the cross. When man in faith submits himself obediently to the command of God, he is ready to receive the divine self-revelation.

God had visibly descended upon the mountain. Moses and the people waited expectantly. The stage was set for the curtain to rise on the next act of the divine drama.

Demands That Call for Obedience
20:1-20

The Ten Commandments are the second major focus of Exodus, along with the Passover account (Ex. 12). They are repeated with a slightly different wording in Deuteronomy (5:6ff.). These Commandments seem to have served as the basis for a major portion of the laws of Exodus. They are certainly the foundation for the ethics of the Old Testament and have made a major impact upon the law codes of the nations of the civilized world.

That there were ten Commandments is unquestioned. Beyond that, however, there are some significant problems. In the biblical text there is no way of distinguishing precisely where each Commandment begins and ends. The Jewish scribes divided the Commandments two different ways. In the Christian communities there are also two basic ways of dividing them. The one with which most of us are familiar (and which we will follow) was accepted by many ancient Jewish authorities, by the early Christian churches, and by most contemporary churches of the Reformed tradition. The Roman Catholics and the Lutherans follow Augustine, combining verses 3 and 4 and dividing verse 17. Regardless of how you divide them, their content remains the same. For Israel, these Commandments were the foundation for their covenant with God.

The Nature of the Covenant (Background)

For centuries, biblical interpreters considered the divine covenant with Israel to be unique. No covenant similar to it was known. Although there were countless covenants mentioned in the Bible and known from the ancient world, these were generally made between two individuals or nations with an essentially equal status to one another. In the Bible, examples of this kind of covenant are seen between Jacob and Laban (Gen. 31:44) and between David and Jonathan (1 Sam. 18:3). Obviously, the covenant between God and Israel was on a totally different basis. In no way could it ever be considered as being between equals.

In recent years, a new study made possible by archaeological discoveries was begun by Dr. George Mendenhall and has shed significant new light upon the form of Yahweh's covenant with Israel. This special study has focused upon the "suzerainty treaties" which were common in the ancient Near East of the second millennium B.C. This kind of treaty or covenant was made between a suzerain ("great king") and his vassal. The suzerain usually identified himself as "king of kings" and "lord of lords." (These titles were picked up later in Revelation 17:14; 19:16 as descriptive of the Lord Jesus.) By these titles, the suzerain claimed ultimate authority over all other kings. In the typical treaty of this nature, several features stood out. Note these as we compare them with the covenant statement in the Bible.

1. The suzerainty treaty began with a statement identifying the great king: "Thus says XYZ, king of . . ." Compare this with "I am the Lord, your God" (20:2).

2. Then followed a statement of the events which led up to and made the treaty possible. These usually emphasized the gracious acts of the suzerain for the vassal. Compare this with "who brought you out of the land of Egypt, out of the house of bondage" (20:2).

3. At this point, the treaty would usually set forth a prohibition against any foreign alliances. This should be compared with "You shall have no other gods before me" (20:3).

4. Following this would be a statement of the covenant obligations for the vassal. Here would be set forth a list of matters which must be done and those which were prohibited. This compares with the rest of the Commandments, setting forth Israel's obligations to God.

5. After this came the statements concerning where the covenant document was to be kept and specifying its public reading. Although this is not contained here in Exodus, it is recorded in retelling this event in Deuteronomy 31:9-11.

6. The typical suzerainty covenant called upon the gods of the great king and his vassal to serve as witnesses. As would be expected, this element is lacking in the Old Testament account of the covenant.

It is worth noting, however, that the prophets regularly called upon the heavens and the earth to serve as witnesses against Israel for having violated the covenant (Isa. 1:2; Jer. 2:12).

7. These treaties usually concluded with a list of blessings and curses that would befall the vassal depending upon whether he remained loyal to the covenant. This compares both with Exodus 23:20-33 and Deuteronomy 27:1 to 28:68.

In this comparison, two things stand out. First, the form of God's covenant with Israel was one with which they were certainly familiar. It was a form with which Moses must have been trained in the palace of Pharaoh. Thus God had begun the preparation of Moses long before Moses ever knew it. The use of this form serves to illustrate again how God frequently takes common things and fills them with uncommon truth. Second, the very use of this form said to Israel, with an unmistakable clarity, that Yahweh was the Great King, the King of kings and Lord of lords. The use of the form itself communicated God's claim to absolute sovereignty over Israel.

Commands Relating to God (20:1-11)

Regardless of how we divide the individual Commandments, it is obvious that they fall into two basic sections. The first Commandments clearly governed the relationship between Israel and God, while the latter ones related to their relationships with one another.

It has been suggested that the Commandments were originally very brief statements, as some of them still are. It is possible that, over the years of God's revelation to and through Israel, some of the Commandments were enlarged, based upon subsequent revelation. The question is really academic. We have no way of knowing what they may have been. We only have them as they are. We must interpret them from this point of view.

Introduction (20:1-2).—The introductory statement points out several fundamental facts. First, the covenant was given by God. Israel did not enter into negotiations with him about it. They could only accept or reject it. In later years they could (and frequently did) break it, but they could not change it. It was never a matter for debate. By accepting the covenant, they were accepting the lordship of Yahweh. If they rejected it, they would have been rejecting his lordship.

Second, the covenant was rooted in Yahweh's historical acts. He was laying claim to Israel's allegiance because he had first redeemed

them. Fundamental to Israel's self-understanding and to their understanding of their relation to God was the fact that he had redeemed
them. Although some have suggested that the covenant was basic
to Israel's faith, it seems more appropriate to recognize that the Exodus was basic to the covenant. While never minimizing the importance
of the covenant, we should never magnify it over God's redemptive
act in the Exodus.

Third, and less significant, Israel was reminded of their heritage
as slaves. They had no greatness to which they could point as a basis
for God's love for them. They were free not because of their power
but because of God's power. There was no basis for pride.

The First Commandment: no other gods (20:3).—Basic to God's
claim upon Israel was that he was to have their sole allegiance. The
word "before" can mean besides or in addition to. We should carefully
note that this Commandment made no claim to Yahweh's being the
only God. That was to come much later in Israel's history. This was
not a statement that other nations did not have other gods, but that
Israel could not do so.

Implicit in this commandment prohibiting other gods was the claim
that "you shall have me." The Hebrews had come out of Egypt, whose
people worshiped large numbers of gods. They were going to Canaan,
where there were an equally large number of gods. That they were
going to be tempted to have many gods is obvious from the fact
that the prophets condemned them for this very sin.

This Commandment speaks to our contemporary culture from two
directions. To those who would seek to place their allegiance in God
and in any other source of power (either real or imaginary), it is God's
demand for a total commitment. On the other hand, for those who
think there is no god at all, it is the divine claim that a person must
have God. There is no real life apart from God.

The Second Commandment: no substitutes (20:4-6).—Let us clearly
recognize that this Commandment was not a prohibition against art-
work but against anything that might take the place of God in Israel's
understanding. In the ancient world, the idolmaker was in many ways
a theologian. His intention was not to say, "My god has the body of
a lion, the legs of a bull, the wings of an eagle, and the head of a
man." Rather, he was saying, "My god has the speed of a lion and
the power of a bull, is exalted as the eagle, and has the wisdom of a
man." With the use of a visual aid, he was trying to describe his

god's attributes. However, the idol worshiper and subsequent idol copiers transferred their worship from the god behind these attributes to the idol itself. The basic thrust of this Commandment, then, was the prohibition against substituting anything for God.

This situation is a real problem in contemporary Christianity. We have a tendency to substitute allegiance to certain words and phrases that describe God for a genuine submission to God himself. Anything, even orthodox descriptions of God, can become an idol. Nothing must be allowed to take God's place in our lives.

The statement that the Lord is a "jealous" God would be better translated as a "zealous" God. This word (which is used only of God) focuses upon an action rather than upon an emotion. It speaks of the fact that God will act to prevent Israel's unfaithfulness or to transform it if it occurs.

"The third and the fourth generation" is a typical expression of the ancient wisdom movement that merely implied continuance. The sins of one generation do affect what follows. However, the real emphasis here was upon God's steadfast love, which was far more extensive than his judgment. It is imperative to note that the demonstrable fact of love was obedience. Biblical love was never an emotion but was always an action. Further, the "love" that God promised is a word always found in the context of the covenant. He committed himself to an unswerving covenant loyalty in his actions.

The Third Commandment: no fruitlessness (20:7).—This is probably the most misunderstood of all the Commandments. The usual interpretation is that it applies to cursing, to the use of some word for God in an expletive. Although it certainly applies to such usage, to narrow its meaning to this alone is almost to misunderstand it completely. Basic to its proper understanding is an understanding of the Old Testament concept of "name," which has been discussed earlier.

In addition, the verb translated "take" means to lift up, bear, or carry. Further, the phrase "in vain" literally means "for nothing" or "for emptiness." In seeking to grasp the meaning of this Commandment, we must also consider the fact that among ancient peoples, divine names were considered to have magical properties.

It would appear that this Commandment was clearly a prohibition against assuming that the mere use of the name of God would produce results. God will not be manipulated by those who seek merely to use his power. Further, anyone who carries about the character or nature of God and has nothing happening in his life has violated this Commandment. The presence of God in anyone's life should produce visible fruits.

He who carries about the nature of God must be a fruitful person. There is no alternative. For anyone who fails to do this, there is the warning "the Lord will not hold him guiltless." This may also be translated, "the Lord will not have made him clean." The very fact of fruitfulness is the evidence of cleansing.

The Fourth Commandment: sanctifying the sabbath (20:8-11).— The longest of all the Commandments, this one also has been frequently misinterpreted. "Remember" should not be translated as an imperative but as a continuing action. The phrase is difficult to translate, but something like this comes close: "Remembering the sabbath day for keeping it holy." As indicated before, that which is holy has been set apart for God. The Commandment states that every seventh day should be set apart for God. A day that is holy is one which is devoted to God's special purposes.

But we must also note that this Commandment governs the use of all time, not just the seventh day. Israel was responsible (as are we) for the use of all the time that God has given. The seventh day was peculiarly devoted to God's service, but all time was a stewardship from him.

The question may be legitimately asked as to why contemporary Christians keep Sunday (the first day) instead of the Jewish sabbath, which is Saturday. The early churches began by keeping the Jewish sabbath and the Lord's Day (Sunday). The Lord's Day was their celebration of the resurrection. In a real sense they celebrated Easter every week. As the gospel spread to non-Jewish peoples, the sabbath was dropped and the Lord's Day was the only day set apart. The Commandment does not necessarily command that Saturday be kept but that one day in seven be set apart especially for God.

We get into a real problem when we try to define how to keep a day holy. Let us recognize immediately that it cannot be done by legislating standards. Jesus established the basic principle when he said, "The sabbath was made for man, not man for the sabbath" (Mark 2:27). The Pharisees had missed the point when they tried to legalize its observance. The day is kept when it glorifies God.

The foundation for the sabbath observance was set in God's creation.

Further, it was he who "hallowed it" or made it "holy." Man's responsibility is twofold. He must demonstrate that he recognizes its holy nature. Further, he must keep all time as God's gift.

Commands Relating to Others (20:12-17)

The first of the Commandments focused upon the vertical dimensions of the covenant, specifying fundamental relations between man and God. The second set turn their attention upon the horizontal dimensions. Here the concern was with the relations that existed between members of the covenant community. These were considered binding only between members of the covenant community, Israel. Although there is an incipient obligation here toward all persons, it was only much later that the Hebrews realized this. In this first formulation they saw only their obligations toward one another. However, with these Commandments they were told that the community had a right to expect and the obligation to demand proper behavior from all who belonged to it.

Although at first glance it may seem that these commands were quite restrictive, we should note that this is not really true. A negative command prohibits only a specific action, leaving all other areas free from restriction. A positive command is far more restrictive, for if you can do only what you are told to do, large areas are left forbidden. The fact, therefore, that all but the first of these last six are negative gave Israel a greater freedom than we might have at first suspected.

The Fifth Commandment: honor to parents (20:12).—This, like the Fourth Commandment, is a positive obligation. Also, like the fourth, it was stated in terms of continuing action. Their lives were to be characterized by honor toward parents. The "honor" expected comes from a word which literally meant to give weight to or to give significance to. The people were expected to recognize the importance of their parents and to make sure that they were put in positions within the community that utilized that importance.

Although we usually seek to limit this as being aimed only at children, this was not the intent at Sinai. Although Paul certainly applied this to children (Eph. 6:2), when it was first given as a part of the covenant it was addressed primarily to the adults of the covenant community. Thus, it was a command to give significance to the old parents—the senior citizens. In many primitive societies, when a person became old and useless, he was sent out to die. It was not to be so in Israel.

The promise connected with this set forth the concept that an enduring society must not only care for its elderly; it must profit from their wisdom. Paul appealed to this promise in his letter to Ephesus (Eph. 6:2-3).

The Sixth Commandment: a right to live (20:13).—This very short command possesses a brevity that belies its significance. The word "kill" is a rare word in the Hebrew. It has been frequently translated as murder. This may be correct. If so, it states that no man can lift up violent hands against another. Certainly the Old Testament never considered this to be a prohibition against capital punishment, for many of the covenant laws have a death penalty. Neither was it considered to be a prohibition against war, for Israel regularly went forth to battle, sometimes at the command of God.

A detailed study of the uses of this word in the Old Testament, coupled with Jesus' further expansion of it in the Sermon on the Mount (Matt. 5:21-22), makes it probable that the word referred to an act of violence that arose out of feelings of hatred or malice. Perhaps murder is the closest word in English, but we must never lose sight of the emotional basis behind the actual slaying.

Regardless of the specific meaning of the verb, the basic purpose of the command was to set forth the sanctity of life. Life was always considered to be God's gift. As such, it was sacred. No man had the right to destroy what God gave.

The Seventh Commandment: faith in marriage (20:14).—Another of the briefer commandments, this marked a major step forward in the understanding of the home. We must note that this prohibited the taking of another man's wife. Certainly it is a far cry from the attitude toward sex taught by Jesus (Matt. 5:27-28). On the other hand, in a time when women were considered as little more than property which could be bought, sold, or taken by force if one could get away with it, this laid a new foundation for marriage. The marriage covenant was to be considered inviolable for people in the covenant community.

It is significant to note just how seriously Israel took this command. Not even the great King David could ignore this command (2 Sam. 11:1 to 12:15). It was also commonly understood that adulterers and murderers were of the same nature (Job 24:13-17). When the prophets

sought for an image to describe Israel's sins against God, they turned
to the image of adultery (Isa. 1:21; Hos. 1:2).

This Commandment called the Hebrews to a purity of life to which
no other people had ever been called. God's people were to live by
a higher standard.

The Eighth Commandment: the right to property (20:15).—The
word used here of stealing implies taking something secretly. Perhaps
it is of significance that each of the acts prohibited by this and the
two preceding Commandments relate to the things done secretly.
In the ancient world (as in the modern), many people believed that
nothing was wrong as long as you did not get caught.

The basic thrust of this Commandment was that property could
not be taken from another. Again, it is important to note just how
important this was considered by the people of Israel. The prophets
had severe words of censure for those who stole the property of others
(Isa. 5:8; Amos 3:10). Property was to be gained by labor, not by
thievery. Stability in a society was (and is) dependent upon security
of life, home, and property.

The Ninth Commandment: the right to truth (20:16).—There is
some question as to the actual meaning of this Commandment. It is
possible that this originally was a statement of the fact that the covenant community had a right to expect and demand truth in legal
matters. If this is correct, then this commandment would have been
limited to a prohibition against lying in legal proceedings. But it is
also possible that this referred to the normal speech of daily life. It
would appear that this would be the more likely meaning, since each
of the other Commandments related to life in the community.

Again, it is fruitless to point out that this was originally limited to
covenant members. This was a major advance over their normal practice. They were not ready yet to receive the full truth which came
only with Jesus. In fact, most of us are not yet ready to hear all the
implications of his teaching. The basic principle for them and for us
is the truth is to be expected. Anything less is too little.

The Tenth Commandment: deliverance from envy (20:17).—It is
possible that the emotion of covetousness dealt with here included
not merely an emotion, but also the active planning of the appropria-
tion of the coveted property. However, the word itself does not necessarily carry this meaning.

Perhaps it is the better part of wisdom to interpret this as being nothing more than what it appears to be—a prohibition against envy. They were not to covet a neighbor's family or his property, or anything else that was his. (Could this have included his good name or his success?)

Ultimately, the foundation of this command was the concept that everything a man possessed was a gift from God. Further, to envy what another had was to despise what you had. Thus covetousness was a rejection of his loving providence.

The Purpose of the Law (20:18-20)

While Moses was receiving the Ten Commandments, the people were perceiving the phenomena that demonstrated the presence of God. Their awareness of his presence struck them with terror, for they "were afraid and trembled" (v. 18). The Hebrew is much more graphic than the English, for the last word literally means that they were staggering or reeling. The awesome holiness of God sent them reeling backward from his presence. If their curiosity had earlier drawn them close to the mountain, the actual presence of God had produced the opposite effect. God at a distance is not as threatening as God nearby.

It is implied that this fear of death had sprung up in them as a response to their having heard the words of the Ten Commandments. The demands of God showed them just how far short of his holiness they were. For the first time they were made to see the real nature of their sin. The awesome light of God illuminated the stain of sin.

Consequently, they desired that Moses should be the mediator between them and God. Knowing their own sinful natures, the people did not wish to hear the voice of God directly. The fear of death at the voice of the holy God is a common theme throughout the Old Testament (Isa. 6:5).

Moses was obviously willing to fulfill the responsibility of mediator. This is the very nature of God's spokesmen. There was both the divine call to service and the human call to intercession. It was certainly because of his earlier call from God that he had been willing to respond to this request of his people.

Moses then offered his people an explanation of God's coming near them. He began by urging them to stop being afraid. God had not come to kill them as a punishment for their sin but "to prove" them. This emphasis upon testing is basic to Exodus. The presence of God was frequently for the purpose of searching out the hearts of men. This knowledge of his testing should serve to help them develop the proper "fear of him" (v. 20). The true fear of God is to be the desire to avoid sin rather than to avoid the consequences of sin.

We must realize that the ultimate purpose of Israel's deliverance from Egypt and of the covenant of Sinai was that they should not sin. God's purposes for Israel were that they should be able to live lives of such quality that they would find it satisfying and fulfilling. The same may be said of the redemptive work of Jesus in our lives. It is his purpose to deliver us from sin and its consequences so that we may really live and not merely exist. This is the good life—the abundant life—in every sense of the word.

Decrees That Govern Life
20:21 to 24:14

This section of Exodus has come to be known as "The Book of the Covenant." This title is based upon the statement that "he took the book of the covenant, and read it in the hearing of the people" (24:7). The section is also frequently called the "Covenant Code," referring to those legal materials basic in Israel's observance of her covenant with God.

As an aid to our understanding of these materials, we need to be aware that many of the laws of this section are not unique to Israel. All the nations of the ancient world were governed by law. Each nation had its own code of laws, all of which possessed both similarities and dissimilarities. This should be expected, for these nations were interrelated over the centuries by commerce, conquest, and migration. Israel was born into this family of nations at Sinai.

Prior to the covenant, Israel had been governed by laws of others as well as their own customs and traditions. Their leader, as a son of Pharaoh, had been educated with the knowledge of Egyptian law and the laws of those nations with whom Egypt was involved. Given this background, it should not prove surprising to find that many of Israel's laws were in similar forms and frequently in the identical words of those of other nations. Under the inspiration of God, the best from the surrounding nations was used with those modifications and alterations made necessary by the fact that Israel was uniquely the people of God. To the laws which had been so selected and modified were added those unique laws which Israel's covenant with God made necessary.

Although not all of the laws in this section are directly related to the Ten Commandments, they are expansions of the basic demands of the Decalogue. They served as the foundation for Israel's faith and life. They governed her worship and her ethics. From the beginning, the people of Israel clearly understood that they were to be a people governed by law. But they also recognized that the laws by which they were to be governed were those of God.

In seeking an understanding of these legal materials, we must beware of trying to interpret them primarily from a Christian point of view. To do so is to miss their essential thrust. We must begin by seeking to understand them against the background of their own time. We must also beware of actually failing to consider them because we find the details foreign and strange.

The Importance of Proper Worship (20:21-26)

Before the actual code of laws which begins in 21:1 ("Now these are the ordinances which you shall set before them"), instructions were given concerning the nature of proper worship. Beginning with a negative command, they were prohibited from making gods of silver or gold. Obviously based upon the Second Commandment, this prohibition covered anything of value. For the Hebrews, gold and silver covered all precious metals. Any type of image would be far removed from the God who actually "talked . . . from heaven" (v. 22). But proper worship involved more than a mere prohibition.

They were given instructions for the making of an altar. Although sacrifice had not yet been regulated or even commanded, it was assumed that Israel would be observing several kinds of sacrifice common in the ancient world. Foreign to our thinking, the ancient sacrificial system was a means by which men expressed their adoration of and gratitude to God. Life was considered sacred. Therefore any animal that was slaughtered was killed in a manner which would express both reverence for life as well as thanks for the gift. The altar itself was to be either of earth or of unhewn stone.

Natural objects were considered to be exactly as God had made them. For man to take the dirt and make mud brick or to take the stone and shape it was to imply that he could do a better job than God had done. Further, both types of altars were easily erected by a nomadic people. Building an altar each time they stopped in the wilderness would have required a period of time and a permanence which they were not to have. It was only after they became a settled people that they were allowed to build a permanent altar.

The prohibition against exposing the sexual organs by climbing the altar is somewhat unclear. Later the priests were commanded to wear "linen breeches." The reference would seem to be of far more significance than merely protecting the priest's modesty. The answer may lie in the fact that in Canaan, to which they were going, the major religion was a fertility cult. The worship was highly sexual. Thus this prohibition may have been a warning against doing anything that might relate to that kind of worship. Whatever the actual meaning, it is obvious that Israel was being told that not only was worship important; *proper* worship was important.

Social Laws (21:1 to 22:17)

The first section of the covenant laws is composed of a miscellaneous collection of what we would call both civil and criminal laws. These were important for the orderly conduct of society. God's people were plainly told that they had responsibilities to and for one another.

The rights of slaves (21:1-11).—To the contemporary mind, the laws governing slavery seem archaic and inhumane. The very idea of slavery is abhorrent to us. To understand these laws, we must see them against their cultural background. Slavery was a cruel but common practice in the ancient world. In that environment, Israel was given a profound truth: *Slaves have rights, too.* Instead of being treated as mere property, slaves were to be considered as persons. Not until long after the coming of Jesus did men realize the ultimate implication of God's love and care and seek to do away with slavery completely. But here was the first step in the long road to the abolition of slavery. Significantly, these laws only governed the rights of Hebrew slaves.

Two sets of laws were given, those governing male slaves and those governing females. The male slave was to be offered his freedom after six years of service. But if he should, because of love and commitment, decide to refuse his freedom, he was to be given the privilege of remaining a slave. This was to be done publicly and to be indicated by a sign that was to have been openly visible. The expression "bring him to God" (v. 6) probably meant to take him to a shrine or sanctuary where God would witness that there was no coercion being exerted.

The female slave was in some ways on a lower level than the male slave, just as a woman in that society was on a lower level than a man. At the same time, because of her lower social status, in many ways there was a greater responsibility toward her. The more unimportant a person was, the greater the responsibility to protect his or her rights. The legal concepts of the Old Testament place a greater responsibility on caring for the weak than for the strong.

The female slave was frequently a concubine and occasionally even a wife. If such a slave did not please her master, he could not sell her to another. He could only let her be redeemed. That is, he could only sell her back to her family. In no way could she be abused or mistreated. Further, if she was so abused, she could go free without the payment of the redemption price.

Capital crimes (21:12-17).—The next set of laws puts forth a series of crimes which were punishable by death. Again, these may appear unduly harsh if judged by Christian standards. On the other hand, these wrong acts were to be taken seriously. Sin must always be taken seriously. Perhaps one of the problems of modern man is that he has taken his wrongdoing too lightly.

The first of these capital crimes was premeditated murder. In order to clarify the nature of the act identified in the basic statement, two explanatory statements were made. To "lie in wait" (v. 13) obviously referred to a planned attack. Such an action would fit into the category of one who "willfully attacks another" (v. 14). This type of killing was considered an act of treachery. It was a betrayal of the common covenant bond that united the people of Israel.

The expression "God let him fall into his hand" (v. 13) is a simple way of saying that the attack was not planned. If the death came as a result of some such accident, the killer could flee to the altar of God. Later, specific cities of refuge were established for such purposes (Num. 35:6). Such a refuge prevented the typical blood feuds that sprang up in the ancient world. Only the guilty should die. This distinction between kinds of killing was a major step forward in the world's laws.

Two of the capital crimes relate to striking (v. 15) or cursing (v.

17) a parent. In the ancient world, words were considered to have an objective reality in themselves. Curses, once spoken, released power and would carry out their work. In the rough society of the ancient world, Israel was being told that order and respect in the home were both important and imperative. Israel's very existence was to depend on obedience and respect within the home.

"Stealing a man" is a way of describing kidnapping. Such practices were fairly common in the ancient world. The slave markets were kept filled by these actions. Even Joseph was so treated by his brothers (Gen. 37). Whether the criminal was found with the victim or merely in possession of the money from his sale, death was to be the penalty. For a man accused of such a crime, unexplained wealth was to be assumed as evidence of guilt.

Israel was being told that the covenant community was to be pure. Crime should not exist in such a community and could not go unpunished.

Ultimately, Israel's legal responsibilities rested upon their covenant with God. With the Exodus, they had been delivered from their slavery to Egypt. With the covenant laws, they were being provided with the first step in their deliverence from sin. This was not completed until the cross. There the ultimate death penalty was paid.

Responsibility for bodily harm (21:18-32).—The set of laws dealing with wounds, blows, and bodily harm is fairly straightforward as far as their obvious meaning is concerned. On the other hand, there are several underlying considerations with which we must deal.

The first concern in the causing of bodily harm was that the injured person be repaid for loss of time and that he be "throughly healed" (v. 19). This presumably referred to complete payment of all medical expenses. However, since medical expenses would have been minimal, it may have only indicated that the obligation for support did not end until there was a complete healing.

Slaves were treated with a different standard. Among the various social strata of that day, slaves were the lowest. In general, they were considered nothing more than property. With these laws the master was told that he had some responsibility toward the slave as a person. Although still considered property, the slave must from thenceforth be considered as a person in some cases. It was a significant step in the right direction for Israel.

The laws regarding miscarriage imply nothing concerning the personhood of the unborn fetus. The punishment stated here was based upon injury to the woman, not to the fetus. The fine was to be suggested by the husband, but must be approved by the judges.

The core of this section was the *lex talionis* or law of retaliation. Certainly Jesus transcended this with his statement of the law of love (Matt. 5:38-39). On the other hand, we can see here a major statement of human responsibility. In much of the ancient world, vengeance was the rule of the day. Here Israel was clearly told that no one could exact more than justice for any injury. This law was intended to prevent excessive punishment for the one causing an injury.

The laws governing injuries to slaves further recognized the personhood of the slave. In other ancient societies, slaves were to be paid for such injuries. In Israel, they were to be given freedom as well.

An ox was considered to be a very dangerous animal in the ancient Near East. The owner was responsible for his ox and for protecting others from it. In some instances, failure to heed this responsibility could even cost the owner his life. However, in such cases, it was possible that the courts could set a sum by which a man might "ransom" his life by the payment of a proper fee of "redemption." These words become very significant in the later thought of salvation. Part of their ultimate meaning becomes clear in their use here.

The price set for a slave, "thirty shekels of silver" (v. 32), has significant overtones for our understanding of the scorn with which the high priest and Judas considered Jesus. The slave was at the lowest rung of the social structure.

The rights of property ownership (21:33 to 22:17).—In this group of laws relating to property rights, some fundamental principles need to be carefully considered. Basic to all of them is that property was important. Ownership of property was recognized as a basic right within Israelite society. But based upon this concept of personal ownership, Israel was given a new development in the common laws of the ancient Near East. The new idea was that loss of property could be made right by equivalent payment. Other ancient law codes provided for vengeful retaliation and even bodily mutilation of the thief or responsible person. The concept of indemnification was similar in purpose to the earlier *lex talionis.* Justice was to be the rule of the day for Israel.

Further, there was also set forth the principle that, as important as property was, human life was more important. In the darkness, a thief might have been accidentally killed. There was no justification for such an act in the daytime.

Animals were the basic source of wealth in a nomadic society. To steal one to kill or sell indicated some degree of premeditation and planning; thus, a major repayment was assessed. While it was also wrong to steal an animal to keep, it was more likely to have been an impulsive act and the fine was not as severe. A man was never allowed to profit from his crime. Upon these principles, these laws themselves can be understood.

The laws relating to one man's animal grazing over the land of another had no real significance for the wandering Hebrews. They owned no land. But it became intensely significant after they entered the land of Canaan. This provision identified precisely the kind of problem faced when a group of nomads were becoming farmers. Further, the problem of fire was of prime significance to Israel after the settlement. The Mediterranean summer was dry, and wildfire could cause untold havoc and loss. He who kindled the fire was responsible for it. The responsibility was there regardless of the intent.

The entrustment or stewardship of another man's property was to be taken seriously. Upon this concept they later developed their belief of the seriousness with which they must take their stewardship of God's gifts. Further, lost property still belonged to its owner. In a case where one man claimed that another had his lost property, both were to be brought "before God." This apparently refers to the taking of an oath in the sanctuary. The priests or elders apparently sat in judgment of such claims. Whoever was found in the wrong was to be treated as a thief by being required to pay double.

The natural dangers of keeping animals in the wilderness were not to be the responsibility of the shepherd. On the other hand, if he allowed an animal to be stolen, he was responsible. Further, though he might not be able to prevent attack by wild beasts, he was responsible for making an attempt to do so. In the event of his failure, he was expected to produce the carcass as evidence.

The set of laws regarding the seduction of a virgin are based upon the premise of the ancients that such a girl was the property of her father. At the time of marriage, he expected to be given a "marriage present" for her. If she were seduced, she no longer had this value. If a man had taken the girl without paying the marriage price, he must do so. The expression "pay money" literally means to weigh silver. Actual money as a medium of exchange had not yet been invented. Payment was made by weighing up a specific amount of gold or silver.

The principles of justice set forth here later served as the basis for the high sense of justice that the prophets possessed. To them, injustice was a sin against God and a violation of the covenant.

Religion and Morality (22:18 to 23:19)

The laws of this part of the covenant code are a miscellaneous collection which related either to religion or morality—sometimes to both. They were probably put together in this collection because of their categorical nature. Only two of the laws in this section are based upon cases. These are stated in the nature of "If . . . you shall . . ." (22:21-24; 23:4-5). The rest are general statements to be universally observed.

More capital offenses (22:18-20).—At first glance, these three offenses seem to be completely unrelated. But they are each aimed at keeping the worship of Yahweh pure.

Sorcery was a common practice in the ancient Near East. Although this specific command was aimed at the "sorceress," the Old Testament also speaks of sorcerers. It would appear that this particular prohibition was aimed at any form of sorcery and thus did not actually exempt men. Throughout the Bible its practice is clearly identified with paganism. Thus the condemnation here was aimed at eliminating paganizing influences in Israel. That it was not completely successful can be seen by the fact that the prophets had to attack the practice later (Isa. 8:19; Mic. 5:12; Mal. 3:5).

Furthermore, there is an obvious difference between "not permit . . . to live" (v. 18) and the expressions "to put to death" (v. 19) and "shall be utterly destroyed" (v. 20). The expression here can be translated as "you shall never allow to live" or as "you shall never allow to begin to live." It would appear that sorcery was to be dealt with drastically. The intent seems to have been aimed at keeping it from getting started and stopping it if it did.

The prohibition against sexual intercourse with an animal was also far more significant than the perversion we normally consider it to be. This practice appears to have been used as a form of magical worship in several nations of the ancient world. Thus this command was aimed not merely at sexual perversion but at false worship. Any such practice was punishable by death.

Finally, any form of open worship to any god other than Yahweh was prohibited. The verb translated "utterly destroyed" has religious overtones difficult to translate. The word refers to the thorough extermination of the offender and all he possessed, since they had been devoted to another god. Both in Egypt, from which Israel had come, and in Canaan, to which they were going, it was common practice to worship many gods. It would have been natural for Israel to have worshiped Yahweh along with other gods. The command was seeking to prevent this practice. That it was necessary can be seen from the fact that Amos, Hosea, Isaiah, and Micah consistently condemned Israel because they tried to integrate the worship of Yahweh with the worship of the Canaanite Baals.

All three commands had the purpose of seeing that Israel's faith remained pure both outwardly and inwardly. Not only were they not to worship foreign gods; they were to avoid anything that might give the appearance of such worship.

Fundamental responsibilities (22:21-27).—Here are a series of responsibilities laid upon Israel relating to the underprivileged in their society. The admonitions may be summed up with the statement that they were commanded to show justice tempered with mercy to the weak, the helpless, and the underprivileged of their society. Although some ancient law codes show similar concerns, in no other instance were these concerns based upon the nature and authority of their gods. Unique to Israel was the expressed concern of their God for such people.

The first such responsibility was directed toward the "stranger." The term used here was aimed specifically at a stranger who was a permanent resident of the community, not one who was just passing through. In the ancient world, strangers seldom had any legal recourse to mistreatment. God reminded Israel that in Egypt they had experienced what could happen to such people. It was to be their responsibility to see that similar things should never happen to anyone who lived among them.

Coupled with the divine protection of the resident alien was God's protection of the "widow or orphan." Without husbands or fathers, such people in the Israelite society belonged to no one and therefore faced extreme hardship. They were consistently considered in the Bible as the most helpless members of society. Their own wives and children would be made widows and orphans. In most ancient societies, the gods were concerned with the strong and powerful. In Israel, God expressed his prime concern with the weak and helpless.

The requirements concerning borrowing and lending give a great deal of difficulty to those who live in our society. In a large measure, society as we know it could not exist without credit, banks, and savings and loan institutions. Are these wrong? Before we can answer that we must consider this command against Israel's cultural background. In Israel's world money was not yet used. Precious metal was occasionally used as a medium of exchange. But most exchange was done by barter (trading one item for another) or by labor (doing a certain amount of work in exchange for some item). This law must be seen against that kind of social structure.

Like the two preceding commands, this law was also aimed at protecting the weak. It prohibited taking advantage of another's misfortune. If disease or a wild animal had killed a man's ox, he would have no way of getting another except by trading sheep for one or working for it. The one furnishing the ox was prohibited from making a profit from his neighbor's misfortune. The word translated "interest" literally means to bite or sting.

Further, in those days, since the community was not settled, there was little which any man (especially a poor man) had in the way of "pledge" or collateral. About the only thing he could part with was his cloak or tunic. It served as his coat in cold weather and as his blanket at night. The creditor was allowed to hold it during the day, but it had to be returned at night when he slept. Obviously, such a practice lessened its value as a pledge. But it did serve as a steady reminder that the debt was owed. It is imperative to note that the basis for this concern for the poor was the fact that God was "compassionate." The word would be better translated as merciful or gracious. Because God was of this nature, Israel was to be also.

Responsibilities in religion (22:28-31).—This series of commands all have specifically religious overtones. Although it may seem strange to us to couple the prohibitions against reviling God and cursing a ruler in the same verse, it is not. In the early days of Israel, the "ruler" appears to have been the tribal chief who was assumed to have been appointed by God. To "curse" such a person would be to curse the one who appointed him. To the Hebrew mind, an attack upon God or upon the divinely appointed leader would have been the same thing—blasphemy.

The next command literally says, "From your fulness and from your outflow, you shall never delay" (author's translation). The "fulness" probably referred to the total harvest of grain and grapes. The "outflow" probably referred to the oil from the olive presses. They were being commanded to bring their offerings from God's abundant blessings at the earliest possible moment. There was never any excuse for delaying the bringing of the offering to God. Although the tithe was practiced earlier (Gen. 14:20) and commanded later (Lev. 27:30), the first officially commanded offerings were these. Obviously, they were expected to bring a proportionate part of their harvest fruit to the God who had given it. The word picture behind the "delay" was the idea of putting off until later. Beginning the process of putting off would merely encourage further and further putting off. This was not to be allowed at all.

The concept of the firstborn belonging to God was common throughout the ancient Near East. This principle was here declared to be binding upon Israel as well. It had been earlier stated (13:2) that the firstborn were to be consecrated to God. Here, as a part of the covenant law, this possession was set forth as an actual gift to God. The later laws add a great deal to this concept, but the principle was always basic to Israel's life.

The fundamental presupposition of all of the covenant law was that the Israelites were to "be men consecrated" to God. They were all responsible for functioning as priests (19:6). As such, they were to abstain from eating anything which had not been properly killed. The blood of an animal, as the symbol of his life which had been given by God, had to be properly handled. The flesh of any animal which had not been so killed was prohibited to them. As men were set apart for God, they had special obligations to fulfill.

Public and private responsibilities (23:1-9).—This seemingly miscellaneous section is bound together by a deep sense of justice. Although other nations in the ancient world at times showed a sense of justice—and although Israel frequently, in actual practice, fell from the commanded ideal—only Israel from the beginning to the end of their history felt a divine compulsion toward justice for all. It was one of their national characteristics. The priests sought it as a matter of course. The prophets proclaimed it. The wise men taught it. God's people were (and are) expected to practice justice.

The first set of stipulations all deal with legal justice, justice within the law courts. It begins with a restatement of the command to truthfulness. The phrase "join hands" refers to the handshake following a legally binding agreement. They were prohibited from entering into such agreements with "wicked" men or from perjuring themselves. They were further admonished against becoming a part of the majority when it was wrong. The will of the mob was never to be confused with justice.

The last of these legal stipulations has given interpreters trouble over the years. They were prohibited from being "partial to a poor man in his suit" (v. 3). In general, we have expected such warnings to be made in the case of great or wealthy men. However, the unexpected here really makes more sense. Everyone was aware of the tendency to be partial to the great man. But the tendency to be partial to a poor man is no less real and far more subtle.

Following these comes a set of commands relating to the treatment of "your enemy's" animals and property. Although these are not specifically related to the courts, there may be a legal background. The "enemy" may be referring to one who is the adversary in a lawsuit. Whether or not this is so, the obvious sense here was that responsibility for justice must always be placed above personal or legal relations. It was not far from this to the concept of "love your enemies" proclaimed by Jesus (Matt. 5:44). The second instance would have required a greater commitment than the first. In the second case, they were commanded to help an animal while the enemy was present. They could not leave "him with it." They had to help "him to lift it up" (v. 5). It is easier to be good to an enemy when he is not around. It is more important when he is.

The stipulations on justice gave the other side of the rich-poor controversy. There is a different word for "poor" in verse 6 than that used in verse 3. The first one merely pointed to the fact that the man was impoverished. The one in verse six is usually used to refer to the "pious poor." Thus this command had the purpose of seeing that a poor man who was in the right got justice.

Israel was also warned against leveling false charges, for such could bring about the death of the one so charged. The term "wicked" here obviously refers to the one who brought such a charge. Bribery was also identified as a corruption and pollution of the cause of justice.

Although Israel had earlier been warned against wronging or oppressing a stranger (22:21), they were here commanded to see that the stranger had the same justice that anyone else got. As a foundation for this command, they were reminded of their own experience in Egypt. History is filled with the stories of oppressed peoples who, when freed, became equally as great oppressors as their own adversaries. Israel was warned against the dangers of this. "You know the heart of a stranger" (v. 9) is certainly not the best translation here. A far better translation would be: "You know the life (or spirit or needs) of a stranger." From beginning to end, Israel was expected to practice justice in all of their dealings.

Religious observances and celebrations (23:10-19).—To us, the sudden shift from justice to religious ritual may seem quite a comedown. In the world in which Israel lived, proper ritual demonstrated a people's devotion to their God. It was based upon the principle that if one was going to serve God, he should do it worthily, in a manner which would bring glory to his name.

The commands concerning the seventh year and the seventh day were based here upon God's concern for the poor, the animals, and the servants. There was an obvious lesson for Israel that they were not the only ones for whom God cared.

The three major sacred festivals were set forth. Passover was not mentioned. This may have been due to the fact that it was assumed to be the first day of "unleavened bread" (v. 15). It may also have been due to the fact that it was primarily a family festival. The "feast of harvest" (v. 16) was fifty days after Passover and later came to be known as Pentecost (from the Greek word for fifty). It was to celebrate the beginning of harvest. The third was the "feast of ingathering" (v. 16) which later came to be known as the Feast of Booths and finally as the Feast of Tabernacles. Although Israel was not yet an agricultural nation, they would become one when they reached Canaan. Such celebrations would be needed and may even have been celebrated by their ancestors in earlier times. They were also similar to such celebrations kept by other agricultural peoples. That is to be expected, since Israel was not born into a religious vacuum.

Blood and fat of an animal were considered to be particularly sacred and had to be handled in special ways. The "first fruits" (v. 19) of the earth were considered to be specially God's, just as the firstborn of man and beast.

The prohibition against boiling "a kid in its mother's milk" was for a long time simply considered to be a prohibition against inhumane practices. However, since archaeologists discovered and translated the great library of Canaanite literature at Ras Shamra, we now know that such a practice was a form of worship to a Canaanite god. Thus this prohibition was a warning against doing anything that might be interpreted as having pagan overtones. It set forth the principle of avoiding any appearance of evil. The concept is still applicable to God's people today.

God's Promised Guidance into Canaan (23:20-33)

Having set forth the basic laws of the covenant, the covenant code comes to an end with a section filled with both promises and exhortations. The basic promises from God concerned his leadership, guidance, fruitfulness, and ultimate victory.

The word translated as "angel" literally means messenger. In the Old Testament, only the context can help us determine whether such a messenger was to have been understood as a supernatural or human leader. In most cases, it is clearly one or the other. In this particular passage, it is not so clearly indicated. God may have been promising an angelic leader or a human one. Either way, the messenger was to be from God and was to guide Israel in following God.

The section also contained some basic warnings. Israel was not to rebel against God's messenger but to hearken to him. They were also warned against having any involvement with the inhabitants of Canaan. That they failed here is amply illustrated by the later messages of the prophets, condemning them for their Canaanite involvements.

The ultimate part of the promise was the assurance of victory coupled with a warning that it would be slow in appearing. God gives his victories on his own time schedule. We are called upon to be obedient and faithful. We can only follow where he leads, waiting for his victory.

The Sealing of the Covenant (24:1-14)

When the laws of the covenant were concluded, Moses was given instructions for sealing the covenant. Such a ceremony was very important, for it gave an outward testimony to the inner commitment to it.

The instructions concerning the persons to be involved were given first. Nadab and Abihu were the two older sons of Aaron. They were intended to follow in their father's footsteps as priests and leaders of Israel. Unfortunately, they failed to be faithful to the Lord and

lost the privilege of service and, ultimately, life itself (Lev. 10:1-2).
The elders were to draw near to God as representatives of the whole
of Israel. Moses was allowed to draw closer than the rest.

Moses came and reported "the words of the Lord and all the ordinances" (v. 3) to the people. The "words" may refer specifically to
the Ten Commandments and the "ordinances" to the rest of the material in the covenant code. However, there may not have been this
kind of division intended here, since in verse 4, "words" seems to
refer to the entire collection. However, later in this same section
(v. 12), God gave Moses the two tablets upon which were apparently
written the Ten Commandments. The entire episode is a bit unclear.
In the ancient world a word or a phrase was used to stand for a
complete sentence or even a paragraph. It is possible that Moses wrote
an abbreviated report which was to serve as a reminder of his entire
oral presentation. The two tablets of stone would have had a detailed
record of the Ten Commandments only.

When Moses reported the words of the covenant, the people committed themselves to it in the same words with which they had made
their earlier commitment (19:8). Their earlier commitment had been
based only upon their knowledge of God. This renewed commitment
was based upon a more detailed understanding of God's demands
and expectations.

The record of the writing of the book of the covenant is the first
record in the Old Testament of Moses writing laws down. We must
remember that in the ancient Near East, oral traditions were the
most common way of passing on a people's history, its faith, and its
cultural heritage. The fact that Moses wrote this down would indicate
that it was considered of supreme importance. It was.

In the ceremony of consecration, two things seem to be of significance. The "young men" served as priests. This was before the setting
apart of a priesthood. Young men would have been needed at this
point to overpower and handle the sacrificial oxen. The other item
of significance was the handling of the blood. Blood was of significance
as the source of life and thus the gift of God. It had to be handled
with particular care. Further, in the ancient world, covenants were
usually sealed by blood. As an indication of how significant it was,
Jesus picked up and developed this concept in the upper room on
the night of his betrayal (Matt. 26:28).

Following the sacrificial ceremony of ratification, there was a communal meal. A meal was eaten only with friends, never with enemies. Thus, the idea of a meal serving as the seal of a covenant arose quite early. (This surely has some overtones for our understanding of the Lord's Supper.) Much has been made of the fact that we are told that "they saw the God of Israel" (v. 10), in relation to Exodus 33:20, "man shall not see me and live." Our understanding must be tempered by the limitations of language and the fact that we have here a human record of a very sacred experience. The actual description clearly shows that they never lifted their eyes. The use of the word "saw" probably meant that they "experienced" God. Much the same meaning is carried when someone suddenly understands an idea and says, "I see."

At the end of the meal, Moses was called higher up the mountain to receive the stone tablets. The later evidence would indicate that these tablets had only the Ten Commandments upon them (31:18; 32:19; 34:1,28). The fact that Joshua was selected to go is an indication of the increasing importance he was being given in Israel.

Worship That Demands the Best
24:15 to 31:18

With this block of material, we approach a section of Exodus which has frequently either been ignored or been misunderstood and misapplied by many Christians. In trying to avoid these two extremes, many students of the Bible have failed to properly appreciate the actual importance of these chapters. Prior to this, we have seen God as the Lord of both history and nature as he prepared Moses, delivered Israel, and led them to Sinai. There he was seen as the absolute Lord of life. From this point, continuing through Leviticus and the early portion of Numbers, God presented himself as the Lord of worship.

There were no atheists in the ancient Near East. Everyone worshiped gods of some kind. Long before the Exodus, Israel's ancestors were worshiping God. Their forms of worship had been similar to and occasionally identical with the worship of their neighbors. With the Exodus, however, they had been given a new experience with

God. They needed new worship forms and facilities to express their new relationship to and new understanding of God. So they were given both new worship forms and new meanings for old forms.

Encounter with God (24:15-18)

Somewhere after having left the elders behind, Moses also left Joshua behind. In the encounter with God, all of the usual manifestations of God's presence were there. The "cloud" and the "fire" were visible testimonies of the experience of God's glory and his voice. The "six days" were apparently days of preparation for Moses. When he was thoroughly ready, when the time was right, God called to him. From a distance, the people could see the cloud and smoke. But they in no way knew what was happening on top of the mountain. As the days dragged on, their anxiety grew until it burst its bounds and overflowed in the experience of the golden calf (Ex. 32).

The Design of the Tabernacle (25:1 to 27:21)

This section deals with the tabernacle, its contents, and how the necessary materials were to be obtained. It has frequently been interpreted in a completely typological manner, seeing every portion of the tabernacle as prefiguring some specific function or aspect of Jesus. Without question, there are many concepts of importance here for understanding the nature and purposes of God. But we must not force the biblical revelation into molds for which it was never intended.

The offerings (25:1-9).—Introductory to the entire section, this passage sets forth how the people were to get the materials that were to be used. The first principle communicated was that the offering was to be completely voluntary, being received from every man "whose heart makes him willing" (v. 2). The word "heart" referred in the Hebrew not to the seat of the emotions but to the seat of thought, purpose, and will. Thus the offering was to come not merely from those who felt like giving, but from those who knew and were committed to the offering as the right thing to do.

Further, those things needed were specified. Some of them were further identified as to their purpose. In general, it would seem that this was done for those objects about which there might have been some question. Also, the ultimate purpose of the offering was specified, that they might "make me a sanctuary." The reason for the sanctuary was stated as being that God might "dwell in their midst" (v. 8). They knew that God was with them at Sinai. The future sanctuary was to be a visible evidence of his continued presence.

Ultimately, the offering was to be used in accord with the directions and purposes of God. It is imperative that God's people use their resources in accord with his will. Nothing less will do. The types of offerings specified here were probably a part of the plunder they took with them when they departed from Egypt.

The interior furnishings (25:10-40).—The objects which were needed for the interior were few but rich. Three were basic: the ark (25:10-22), the table (25:23-30), and the lampstand (25:31-40).

The ark was a small box to be overlaid with gold. (A cubit was the length from the tip of the fingers to the elbow, about eighteen inches.) The method of carrying it was intended to prevent anyone from ever actually touching the ark itself. The "mercy seat" comes from a Hebrew word that literally means to cover. However, the word is consistently used in the Old Testament with the theological concept of God's covering or atoning for sin. Thus it is here translated as "mercy seat" rather than by its more ordinary function of serving as a cover for the box. On the top of the lid were soldered two small cherubim. These were apparently winged sphinxes with human faces. They were regularly considered to be symbolic of the messengers and attendants of God. Later, in the Temple, two gigantic cherubim were erected (2 Chron. 3:10-13). In the ark was to be placed "the testimony" (v. 22). This referred to the two stone tablets with the Ten Commandments. The entire box was to serve as a symbol of the place where God would speak with Israel.

There was also to be a table just as luxuriously finished as the ark. The table was also to be portable. It was designed to hold the utensils used in worship. There were "plates and dishes" used for the incense offerings and "flagons and bowls" (v. 29) used for the drink offerings. The "bread of the Presence" (v. 30) was twelve flat cakes (Lev. 24:5-6) which were set out fresh each morning and were removed each evening. Although the symbolism was not specified, this bread was apparently to represent the presence and providential care of God.

The final object of furniture was to be the lampstand. This was the Menorah, which is still one of the basic symbols of modern Judaism. The lamps upon the stand were primarily present for their practical value. They were to give light (v. 37) to the holy place within the tabernacle. In later days, the light from the lamp came to symbolize God's presence. Further, the symbolism of "seven" lamps was that of the sacred nature of the light that was to be furnished.

The beauty of the design and the worth of its content was surpassing. It is difficult to determine the actual weight of a talent. It seems to have varied from time to time. It was the largest measurement for weight used in Israel and varied from about 70 to about 130 pounds. The lampstand itself with its branches and leaves apparently symbolized a tree. The almond tree later served as a reminder to Jeremiah that God was watching over his people (Jer. 1:11-12).

A final warning was given to Moses to see that all of the furnishings were made in accord with God's directions. It was imperative that God's people follow his plans in fulfilling their divinely appointed tasks. The worth of the furnishings served as an obvious reminder that they were to use their very best in his service.

The tabernacle itself (26:1-37).—The outline of the tabernacle itself was determined by the wooden frames. It was thirty cubits on a side (twenty frames of one and one-half cubits each) and about nine cubits on each end (six frames of one and one-half cubits each). The walls were ten cubits high. The rear wall was actually wider at the bottom than at the top, due to the shaping of the corner frames (vv. 23-24). The rear third of the tent was set apart from the holy place. It was called the "most holy" place, and later came to be known as the holy of holies. The luxurious wall hangings were on the interior only, with a roof and exterior covering of normal tent cloth. The holy place was lighted by the lamps upon the lampstand. The most holy place was totally dark. It contained only the ark, with no auxiliary lamps.

The altar, courtyard, and lamp oil (27:1-21).—The altar itself stood outside the tabernacle proper and was made of wood overlaid with bronze. The horns were small projections on each of the four corners. The altar was hollow to make it easier to carry. In use, it was probably filled with earth to keep the wood from burning.

The courtyard of the tabernacle was set off by curtains to isolate the area in front of the tabernacle, which was considered to be holy. The east wall was not completely enclosed, but the opening was filled in with a screen so that it would not be open to profane viewing. Although the exterior vessels and screening were not of the same luxury as that of the interior, they were extremely well appointed.

The final provision was not for the furnishings but for the oil that would be used for the lampstand in the holy place. Only the purest of olive oil was good enough for God's service. There was a further admonition that the lamp must burn continually.

The entire complex was designed to proclaim to Israel the abiding presence of God and to demand from them, in response, faithful, obedient service. Its portability indicated that God and they were going to be on the move. They were being led to a land beyond. The wilderness was not their home; nor was it his.

The Priestly Robes (28:1-43)

The priestly robes were described in detail, but some of the references are unclear to us since we are so far removed from the times. The garments were to be "holy" or set apart from ordinary clothing. The purpose of the garments was that they should be "for glory and for beauty." Thus they probably symbolized the social status and rank of the priesthood as well as their particular relation to God. Aaron's garments, which were for the high priest, were much more ornate than those of his sons, who were just ordinary priests.

The "ephod" may have been a vestlike garment supported by two straps that were fastened at the shoulder by two stone clasps, which were engraved with the names of the tribes of Israel. Thus, when the high priest was serving in the tabernacle, he was symbolically bearing about with him the entire nation of Israel in their tribal names.

The "breastpiece of judgment" was a small pouch hung across the priest's chest. It was so called because in it were the sacred lots, "the Urim and the Thummim" (v. 30). These names literally mean "the Lights and the Perfections." There were probably intended to describe the nature of the God whose will they were thought to reveal. The Bible has numerous instances where such sacred lots were used to determine the will of God. The pouch in which they were kept was the lodging place of the judgments of God. The pouch was decorated with twelve stones which served the same purpose as the two stone clasps of the ephod.

The golden bells on the skirts of the priestly robes were intended to ring as the priest moved about in the holy place, carrying out his functions. This allowed the people outside to know that the priest was not dead. That he was alive and moving demonstrated that their offering had been accepted by God.

The "pomegranates" (v. 34) were ancient symbols of fruitfulness.

Whether they had that meaning here or were merely decorative is unclear. Most likely, they were intended to represent Israel's fruitfulness as a gift of God.

The golden plate upon the turban was engraved with the motto "Holy to the Lord" (v. 36). It was symbolic of Israel's offering to God. It had the purpose of making them acceptable before God.

Inserted near the end of the description of the priestly garments was the command to "anoint them and ordain them and consecrate them" (v. 41). Anointing was done with holy oil and served to set apart that person (or thing) specifically to God's service. "Ordain," as used here, literally means "you shall fill their hand." The reference probably meant to put in his hand the tasks of the priesthood, to pass on to them the responsibilities which God had given. The consecration was a technical term meaning to make holy. It was to set someone apart for the specific service of God. Each of these terms underlines the fact that the priests were set apart for God's service.

Following the description of the plain garments of the ordinary priests was the specification of the "linen breeches." This was obviously an early form of underwear. It was probably designed to indicate that Israel's worship was in no way to be similar to the fertility cults of the surrounding nations. Whereas the other nations played up the sexual nature of their worship, Israel demonstrated that their worship had no sexual overtones at all.

The Consecration of the Priests (29:1-46)

The setting apart of the priests for the service of God involved a great deal of ritual which was similar to that of most peoples of the ancient Near East. There were some basic principles which were of permanent significance. The ceremonies of washing, cleansing, anointing, and offering the special sacrifices were performed to show that a priest could not lead others further in the service of God than he had gone himself. Further, in order to serve God, one must be both clean and pure, as well as being set apart by God.

The first step in the process involved the ceremonial washing away of all that was unclean. Although the meaning changed over the centuries, this was probably the forerunner of Christian baptism. The priesthood was to belong to the family of Aaron by a "perpetual statute" (v. 9).

The animal sacrifices were of three types: a sin offering, a burnt offering, and a wave offering. The sin and the burnt offering were common offerings and were used throughout Israel's history for persons other than priests. The final offering, though similar to other wave offerings in the Old Testament, was specifically designated as the offering of ordination.

Each of the offerings had a separate meaning for the priests. The sin offering was intended to be symbolic of the cleansing of their sins. The burnt offering, which was wholly consumed, was symbolic of their total devotion to the will and service of God. That they laid their hands upon the heads of these animals showed that they were identifying themselves with them. With the wave offering for ordination, there are other symbols present. The blood was used in the sense of life. Touching it to the ear, thumb, and toe showed that God had given special life to these organs. The priest was to hear and obey the voice of God, while his hands and feet were to be devoted to the divine service.

The wave offering was done by moving the portion of the animal toward the altar and then away from it, rather than in a right-to-left motion. The apparent symbolism was that this was being offered to God and then being given back to the priests by God. Throughout Israel's history these portions were the payments of the priests. They were their "perpetual due from the people of Israel" (v. 28).

The "seven days" devoted to the ordination of the priests here was probably quite literal, although it certainly carried the idea that they were totally and completely devoted to God. The seven days of ordination were probably also to signify that every day of the week was to be devoted to their service of God. During this ceremony, not only were the priests sanctified; the altar was also sanctified.

Following the commands specifically designated for the consecration of the priests, the laws concerning the daily sacrifices were given. These later came to be the heart of the Hebrew sacrificial system. The purpose of these daily sacrifices was set forth as indicating that as Israel presented her sacrifices at the door of the "tent of meeting" (another name for the tabernacle), so God would meet with them and reveal his word to them.

It is imperative for us to note that Moses, the priests, and Israel were just going through the symbols. The actual consecration of both objects and persons was done by God. His grace made them effective. The purpose of this ritual and this consecration was that God would "dwell among the people of Israel" (v. 45). This ritual was to help them know that he was the God who had redeemed them from Egypt. The final phrase "I am the Lord their God" (v. 46) is uniquely a covenant phrase. Because they were his people through the Exodus and the covenant, they had a special ritual of worship.

Other Worship Objects (30:1-38)

The basic idea which binds these instructions together is that they are all related to the worship of Israel. Although they are diverse otherwise, this common concern caused them to be placed together.

The altar of incense (30:1-10).—This altar was a smaller version of the larger altar of sacrifice in front of the tabernacle. As was true of the other objects, this too was to be portable. It stood in the holy place in front of the veil that shut off the most holy place. Twice daily incense was to have been burned upon this small altar. The purpose was apparently to send up a cloud of smoke which was to remind Israel of the presence of God. It was imperative that nothing be offered upon this altar except that which was specifically required.

The "horns" of the altar were four small projections on each of the upper corners. The ceremony of annual atonement for the altar is probably to be understood as a part of the ritual of the great Day of Atonement (Lev. 16; 23:26-32). The atonement for the altar was due to the fact that it belonged to a sinful people. In the Old Testament, objects were considered to have qualities which we attribute only to people in modern times.

The census tax (30:11-16).—Whenever Israel took a census, they were supposed to pay a tax to the sanctuary. This was "for the service of the tent of meeting" (v. 16). The occasion of such censuses was left unspecified. It was such a census that gave the book of Numbers its name (Num. 1) and the apparent disregard of the tax that created problems in David's time (2 Sam. 24). Since the people of Israel were God's army, a census may have been needed in times of crisis to determine the availability of fighting men. At these times, since Israel as a whole was God's firstborn, each man needed to be ransomed. This was before the times of coined money, so taxes were assessed by weight. The "shekel of the sanctuary" was a standard weight, equivalent to about two-fifths of an ounce.

The bronze laver (30:17-21).—The size of the bronze laver was not given, but it was apparently rather small. It held water for the ceremonial cleansing of the priests before they entered the tent of meeting or before they offered a sacrifice upon the altar. The cleansing, however, was obviously of practical value, for the priest would certainly need to wash his hands after slaughtering a sacrificial victim. The expression "lest they die" clearly indicated that those who served in holy worship must be clean. The outer cleansing was symbolic of inner cleanliness.

The anointing oil (30:22-33).—The anointing oil was intended to set an object or a person apart to God. The amount of holy oil to be prepared would have been quite large. A "hin" was approximately one gallon. The total amount prepared would have been about thirty-eight pounds plus the weight of a gallon of olive oil. To use this for any purpose other than that specified was considered to invite punishment by death, for this appears to be the meaning of "be cut off from his people" (v. 33).

The incense (30:34-38).—The incense is described as "most holy." The apparent contrast between this and the "holy" oil was that the incense was to be used closer to the ark and therefore closer to God. The recipe clearly calls for rare spices, although not all of them can be presently identified. Frankincense is regularly identified as quite valuable. The addition of "salt" is an intriguing idea. The salt may have been nothing more than a preservative, but that seems unlikely. The fact that sharing "salt" between two people was considered to bind them in a covenant was probably the basis of this command. Israel's "salt" was offered to their God. This was probably considered their seal upon the covenant relation that God offered. As in the case of the oil, violation of the rules for the use of the incense was punishable by death.

God's Skilled Craftsmen (31:1-11)

Having specified the tasks which had to be performed in the construction of the sacred objects and vestments, God then indicated that he had appointed two men as leaders and others as helpers in accomplishing these tasks. The name Bezalel means "in God's shadow," while Oholiab means "my tent is the Father." Both names show that their parents found sustenance in the presence of God. This heritage surely must have made an impact upon these men.

Both men had been given special gifts by God to enable them to accomplish the tasks about to be set before them. Bezalel, the apparent leader, as he was listed first and with much greater qualifications, was said to have been filled with "the Spirit of God." As evidence of this special filling, he had been given "ability," "intelligence," "knowledge," and "craftsmanship" (v. 3). In all likelihood, these were skills that he had used while a slave in Egypt. God had obviously prepared far in advance of the particular need that now arose.

In addition to the two leaders, God had given other abilities and skills to other men that they might be utilized in doing the works necessary for the preparation of the tabernacle and its appointments. But not only had they been given the skill; there was a promise from God that they would be faithful and obedient in completing the tasks assigned. "According to all that I have commanded you shall do." (v. 11). In the Old Testament, faithfulness and loyalty were considered to have been gifts of God.

The Sabbath Observance (31:12-17)

A fairly constant thought in the Old Testament was the fact that the sabbath observance was considered an outward sign of Israel's covenant commitment. It was a sign that God had set them apart for himself. The death penalty here pronounced upon violaters of the sabbath laws shows how seriously they were to take it. Although it was apparently not enforced with any regularity, it was enforced once in the wilderness (Num. 15:32-36). It also served as the basis of an early attempt to execute Jesus (John 5:16-18).

The basis for keeping the sabbath was again set forth as the rest of God from his creation activities. As a memorial to God's creative activity and as a permanent sign to their covenant relation, they were to keep the sabbath. For the Christian, the one day in seven which we observe stands as a memorial to the resurrection that symbolizes God's new creation in Christ Jesus and to our new covenant with him.

The Tables of the Testimony (31:18)

When Moses had been given all the instructions needed for the preparation of Israel's worship facilities, God gave him "the two tables of the testimony." It is probable that these two tables contained neither the stipulations for the worship materials nor the Covenant Code, but merely the Ten Commandments. When he replaced them after having destroyed this original set, the tables of the testimony obviously contained only the "ten commandments" (34:28-29). In fact, in that place, the expression "ten commandments" literally reads "ten words." It is therefore quite likely that the original written version of these Commandments was very brief, probably containing nothing but the basic statement of each commandment.

The expression "written with the finger of God" might offer a possible problem. It may be quite literal. Therefore God would have actually written upon the tablets of stone. On the other hand, the expression "This is the finger of God," as used in 8:19, would indicate that the expression may have referred to the power of God at work in and through a dedicated human (Moses, in that case). Further, when the tablets were replaced, God told Moses, "I will write upon the tables the words that were on the first tables" (34:1). But when it was actually accomplished, it was done by Moses at God's command (34:27-28). Either way, the point is the same: The message came from God and with his authority.

While Moses was on the mountain, there had been an extended period of revelation from God. How it came about is immaterial. Certainly Moses came to that place with all sorts of experience upon which God could and probably did draw. While he was being trained in Egypt, Moses would have learned the law codes of Egypt and those nations with whom she was involved. He also would have known a great deal about Canaan, toward which they were going, for Canaan was a tributary of Egypt at that time. With that knowledge, Moses could offer to God a fertile seedbed for the revelation of what Israel was to do and to be in the light of the world in which they existed. In whatever ways God may have used Moses' knowledge and training, it is sure that our God never wastes any part of man's experiences.

Renewal That Follows Rebellion
32:1 to 34:35

The narrative events of this section were beginning to develop while Moses was on the mountain with God. The basic theme is common to the Old Testament: rebellion, restoration, and renewal. The basic question posed and answered by these events was simple: "Is there mercy and forgiveness for stubborn rebels just as there was

deliverance for helpless slaves?" The answer came forth with a re-
sounding "Yes!"

Further, if ever there were any doubt as to the basic character of
Moses, it was thoroughly removed in these events. He resisted the
temptation of selfish pride and stepped forth as the great intercessor
of the Old Testament. He showed himself to be one who was totally
devoted to the people and ministry to which God had called him.
His anger was violent. But its violence sprang from his love, not from
any baser emotion.

Rebellion in the Presence of God (32:1-35)

The narrative we have followed had left off when Moses had gone
up the mountain to God, disappearing within the smoke and cloud
(24:15-18). During the time he was on the mountain, the people were
waiting at its foot. The emotions of the Hebrews had been stretched
to the breaking point. There had been the constant up and down
experiences in Egypt. This had been followed by the despair and
deliverance at the sea. On the heels of this had come the high and
low moments of the wilderness, as well as the exhausting experience
of their journey to the mountain. This had led to the terrifying and
wonderful confrontation of the giving of the covenant.

Suddenly their leader disappeared. They may have waited patiently
for a few days; but, as the time of Moses' absence was drawn out,
the people became restless. They were used to excitement. The sudden peace and calm of the desert began to hang heavy. Further,
there was the growing fear that something might have happened
to Moses. Against that background, we will examine their rebellion.

The demand for a god (32:1-6).—The story began on the level of
human impatience. When God was not doing something visible, they
assumed he was not there. They failed to accept what God had done
for them. Their almost contemptuous description of Moses as "the
man who brought us up out of the land of Egypt" showed that they
had failed to recognize that it was God who had redeemed them.

Further, there was a total lack of trust. Their statement "we do
not know what has become of him" (v. 1) clearly demonstrated their
lack of concern for Moses and their lack of trust in God. The God
who had constantly led and rescued them could have taken care of
Moses on the mount.

Israel wanted a leader they could see. They did not feel that they
could get along without something tangible to guide them. Their

approach to Aaron gave him a real opportunity for leadership. At the least, he could have reminded them of the law prohibiting idols. At the best, he could have exhorted them and led them away from the evil they were planning. He did neither. Instead, he submitted to their request and became a leader in their apostasy. Like so many after him, he chose the popular instead of the prophetic way.

The nature of the "molten calf" (v. 4) that he made is somewhat in doubt. The immediate impression was that it was solid gold which was molded and then carved into its precise details. However, the fact that it could later be burnt and then its residue "ground . . . to powder" (v. 20) would indicate that it could possibly have been a wooden carving overlaid with gold. They certainly had adequate skills to do either. Further, the latter technique was the one later used in constructing the ark and much of the tabernacle.

The word "calf" would be better translated as "bull." The choice of a bull to represent their God was probably based upon the Canaanite Baal worship. The Baals were frequently represented by the figure of a bull. It is also known that Baal worship was practiced by Semitic slaves resident in the delta region of Egypt. When the Hebrews saw the bull, they saw it as symbolic of their "gods." Two things stand out in that declaration. First, they were not yet convinced that God was the only God for them. Second, neither were they convinced that they should not worship an image. We need to remember that they were fresh from slavery. Their newfound freedom was more than they had yet been able to cope with.

The greatest tragedy was the fact that they gave credit to their handmade god for their deliverance from Egypt. It was a sad day for Israel. Giving credit for God's acts of mercy to some other force or power is a frequent temptation. It is difficult for us to understand their worship of the gods for whom the bull stood. But we too face the ever real temptation to serve things for their real or imagined power. Although somewhat more subtle, such service is little different from Israel's rebellion.

When Aaron saw that the people were going to worship the bull, he "built an altar before it" (v. 5). This was apparently an earthen altar or an altar of loose stones. No sudden burst of misguided exuberance led them to worship the golden bull. The time and effort needed to erect an altar demonstrate that there was some organization to their idolatry.

Some have suggested that Aaron's proclamation that "tomorrow shall be a feast to the Lord" (v. 5) was a brave attempt to salvage something of worship to Yahweh out of this rebellion. There is no indication that the Old Testament ever took any such view of his action. It is far more likely that he was merely identifying the God of Israel with Baal. Such identification and syncretism was precisely what the prophets attacked so vehemently in Israel's subsequent history. Open rebellion was viewed with less hostility than this kind of consolidation. This approach says that all gods are alike. To the contrary, the Bible clearly states that the God of Israel is unique.

On the day of the great celebration, they offered the typical offerings common throughout the ancient Near East, the "burnt offerings" and the "peace offerings." This set of sacrifices was followed by the typical communal meal. Following this, they "rose up to play" (v. 6). This expression suggests the type of sexual orgies that accompanied the worship in the Canaanite fertility cults. That these cults were dedicated to the Baals is another indication that the "bull" was probably to be identified with the Baals of Canaan.

Such a manner of worship appealed to the basest aspects of human nature. That it was ascribed to the worship of the God of Israel who in the Ten Commandments had revealed his moral nature was both unbelievable and an unbearable insult. It could go neither unnoticed nor unpunished.

Judgment and mercy (32:7-14).—The scene shifts abruptly from the lighthearted merrymaking in the valley to the heartbreak on the mountain. God informed Moses of the sin of Israel, breaking into their communion with the abrupt command, "Go down." The contrast between the two scenes makes the spiritual gulf all the more real.

The change in pronouns is also emphatic. *"Your* people, whom *you* brought up out of the land of Egypt, have corrupted themselves" (v. 7, author's italics). Israel had repudiated God; now God was repudiating Israel. Such is always the way with sin.

Israel's rebellion had many dimensions. They had "corrupted" themselves. This referred to the marring, spoiling effects of sin. They had "turned aside quickly." It was not a gradual drift away from God but a sudden, deliberate choice. They had made a "molten calf," which was a deliberate violation of the covenant. They had given credit to the idol for doing what God had done. Such was the nature of Israel's sin. It resulted in God's description of them as a "stiff-necked people." This was a common Old Testament description which would have been familiar to people who dealt with large farm animals. It was descriptive of an ox or an ass which would not respond when the rope around its neck was tugged. It reflects a stubborn disobedience.

God then revealed himself in a divine paradox. At the same time he put Moses to the test. At first reading, verse 10 reflects the all-consuming "wrath" of God about to issue in judgment. But a second reading shows that the promised judgment was made conditional upon Moses' agreement, for God said, "Now therefore let me alone" (v. 10). God himself left the door open for intercession and therefore for mercy.

The test to Moses was couched in words identical to the earlier promise to Abraham (Gen. 12:2). The temptation to Moses was whether he would abandon his call to lead Israel and turn aside from his faith in the divine promises. Needless to say, God already knew what kind of man Moses was. But God regularly calls upon his saints for a public demonstration of those inner qualities of commitment.

Moses responded to God in one of the most profound intercessory prayers in the Bible. Perhaps one of the secrets of Moses' real greatness can be found in such prayers. Moses based his prayer upon three specific appeals. First, there was the appeal to the fact that God had redeemed Israel with "great power and a mighty hand" (v. 11). He appealed to God not to repudiate his mighty acts. There was also the further play upon the pronouns, as Moses referred to Israel as "thy people." Second, Moses appealed to the consequent scoffing of the Egyptians if Israel were destroyed. Third, he appealed to the divine promises to "Abraham, Isaac, and Israel." There was no appeal to the fact that Israel should be spared either for any worth or merit on their part or on the part of their forefathers. The fundamental basis for the appeal was the very nature of God. He had promised. He would be faithful.

The end result of the intercession of Moses was that "the Lord repented of the evil which he thought to do to his people" (v. 14). The word used in the Old Testament for the divine repentance is not the same word used for human repentance. This word has no connotation of guilt or a change of purpose because the first was wrong. Rather, it is essentially a word of deep feeling, implying the choice of an alternate course of action. We must recognize that Moses had not overpowered God's unwillingness to spare Israel. Instead, he had seized upon God's desire to be merciful. Guilt must be punished. But it was the fact that God's inherent nature is merciful which Moses both recognized and claimed. Further, if there was ever any doubt as to whether Moses had become enamoured with his own importance, his intercession here dispelled all doubts. He had been called to lead Israel. He would not forsake them for his own glory. Such was the measure of his commitment to both God and Israel.

Decision and mediation (32:15-35).—As Moses went down from the mountain, he carried the tables of the law with him. There is no way to judge the size of the tables, but it is quite likely that the usual artist's representation of them is far too large. That would have created a tremendous burden and made it very difficult for Moses to climb down the mountain. Further, the fact that the tables were written upon both sides would also have indicated that they were small.

When Moses "broke" the tables, several factors were involved. It was an outward expression of his anger at the sin of the people. Far beyond that, however, it was intended as a visible sign that Israel had broken the covenant. Therefore the tables that symbolized the covenant were broken. Further, it was a clear testimony that they had completely repudiated the work of God. As the tables were the "work of God" (v. 16), either actually or based upon his authority and power, so was the covenant they had broken.

The burning of the calf and the grinding of the residue probably reflects the fact that the idol was a wooden frame overlaid with gold. Following the burning, there would have been the leftover gold which could have been ground up. This, along with the ashes, was mixed with water and given to the people to drink. This has often been considered to be related to the "water of bitterness" used as a test for a wife's fidelity in Numbers 5. There is no biblical evidence that it should be so understood, although the fact that Israel had been unfaithful to her God makes it an attractive interpretation. It is more likely that this was merely a way of punishing Israel as well as completely getting rid of the idol.

The conversation between Moses and Aaron was quite humorous, even though it was also tragic. The nature of Moses' question implied that he found it inconceivable that Aaron could have participated in such a sin without major threats or pressure. Aaron's excuse took two avenues. He first blamed the people and then ultimately blamed

Moses for staying on the mountain so long.

His second avenue of excuse was to imply some sort of miraculous event. To worship the work of our own hands is foolish. To imply that it created itself is even more so. Moses did not waste time seeking to argue with Aaron. One mark of the authenticity of the story is that it is in the Bible at all. No one would ever have invented such a story about the first high priest of Israel. Even if Aaron's excuse had been true, the fact that he had allowed them to "break loose" (v. 25) was also an evidence of his guilt. For the biblical writer, a failure to act could also be a sign of guilt.

At this point Moses issued his call to decision: "Who is on the Lord's side?" (v. 26). Literally, the Hebrew says: "Who is for Yahweh?" The call was for a specific choice, an act of will. Although not everyone may have been involved in the idolatrous worship, there is no record of any opposition. With Moses' question, there was no opportunity left for sitting on a fence. The time had come when they had to take a stand. The fact that only the sons of Levi responded shows just how widespread the crisis was. It also made Aaron stand out as a great failure. Even those in his own clan were more loyal than he.

The execution of "about three thousand men" (v. 28) has offered some problems in interpretation. First, it is obvious that not everyone who was involved was executed. Apparently those who were executed were a random selection. The fact that most were allowed to live stands out as an example of mercy in a day when infidelity was considered to be a capital crime. Second, the difficulty of the task for the sons of Levi was apparent. The call of God does not always lead to pleasant paths. There was to have been no partiality in the execution of judgment. Third, the carrying out of the death sentence shows just how seriously they regarded apostasy. It was not dealt with lightly.

We must beware of seeking to evaluate their actions on the basis of New Testament ethics. If we are going to understand this event, we must do so against the background of their own culture. Their sin was dealt with in a rough harshness. But it was tempered by mercy beyond that of the surrounding cultures.

The expression "you have ordained yourselves" literally means "filled your hands." It was a way of expressing that they had filled their hands voluntarily and obediently with the service of God. That they had been willing to do this served as the foundation for their future use as leaders in Israel's service of God.

Following the day of judgment and mercy, Moses went back to God as an intercessor and mediator. "Perhaps I can make atonement for your sin" (v. 30) literally means "perhaps I can cover for your sin." Moses was going to try to do superficially what only Jesus does fully. Moses' great intercessory prayer sought to lay hold of God's mercy. In it, he offered to die alongside of or in place of his people. God did not allow Moses to do what only he could ultimately do. It was in Christ Jesus that he himself would die for the sins of his people.

Instead, Moses was told that their sin must be punished. On the other hand, God did reiterate his promise that Israel could go on to the land of promise. Further, there would be the guidance of the angel of God along the way. They would not be left to fend for themselves.

"Thy book" (v. 33) presupposed a book of life that God was keeping, the first mention of this concept in the Bible. It was referred to later in Psalm 69:28; Isaiah 4:3; Philippians 4:3; and Revelation 3:5.

The "plague" which was sent is otherwise unidentified. It may have been some sort of illness. Whatever it was, it was clearly understood as having come in direct consequence of their disobedience.

Grace and Glory (33:1-23)

In the repeated command to go on toward Canaan, we should not see so much an order to immediately depart, but an assurance that God would ultimately keep his promise. They did not actually depart from Sinai until after the complete giving of the law (Num. 10:11-12). God promised to send his "angel" as a guide. The Hebrew word for angel can also be translated as messenger. This is how it should probably be understood here, since Moses later said, "Thou hast not let me know whom thou wilt send with me" (33:12). At this point, the guide was unidentified. The emphasis was upon the fact that the guide was a substitute for the direct, personal presence of God. The reason given for this was that it was not so much designed to punish as to protect Israel, "lest I consume you in the way" (v. 3).

The removal of the "ornaments" was a sign of mourning as well as a sign of obedience. It is possible that the ornaments may have been religious medallions of some sort. Archaeologists have uncovered many such. On the other hand, these may have been put away since it was from such ornaments that they had made the idol. In this case they would have been removing the temptation to repeat that sin. Whatever the reason, the ornaments were put aside in obedience. It certainly set Israel apart from the nations of the ancient Near East. There was now an external, visible difference between them and their neighbors, which reflected their relation to God.

The passage dealing with the "tent of meeting" was put in to further emphasize that their sin had caused a distance to be put between them and God. No longer was God in the midst of Israel. In order for a man to seek Yahweh for any reason, he had to physically separate himself from the rest of his people. There is a principle implied here that man must approach God by drawing apart from the world for a season. Furthermore, a related emphasis was placed upon the fact that Moses enjoyed a closer relationship with God than the others. The Lord spoke with Moses "face to face, as a man speaks to his friend" (v. 11). This expressed the real depth of the communion between Moses and God.

No reason was given for the fact that Joshua remained behind in the tent after Moses departed. The only thing we can safely say at this point is that it is obvious that Joshua had become Moses' close assistant instead of Aaron. Aaron had forfeited that right by his sin with the golden calf.

Based upon the close relationship that has been described, Moses pled with God for additional assurance. It is not clear whether Moses was asking specifically to know who would go with them as guide or whether he was seeking indirectly for an assurance that God would go with them. "Show me now thy ways" (v. 13) could have simply been a request for a road map. More likely, it was a request for an additional revelation of the purposes of God.

Whatever Moses was asking for, God assured him of two things, his "presence" and his "rest." Again, Moses' intercession had laid hold of God's willingness. The "rest" of God was a sense of security and peace rather than a cessation from labor. It was basically an inner rather than an outer experience.

For Moses, the assurance of God's presence was that which would make Israel distinct from all her neighbors. He never questioned that they should be distinct. But he plainly knew that ultimate distinctiveness rested upon their relation with God. If that were gone, all other distinctives would have been superficial.

Following this assurance, Moses prayed for a special, unique vision

of God. The word "glory," as used here, referred to the actual presence
of God. Moses was first given an inner revelation of God, that God's
real nature was that of grace and mercy. The real glory of God is
seen not in a form but in the experience of his gracious mercy. Grace
is the real evidence of the glory or presence of God. But then Moses
was assured that the holiness of God was such that no one could
really see him and live. Man can only see where God has been. The
description of looking upon God's "back" was a picturesque way of
describing the fact that our best view of God is found in seeing what
he has done and where he has been. This was precisely what Jesus
said to messengers of the imprisoned John the Baptist. He told them
to report what they had seen going on (Matt. 11:2-6). It is in the
actions of God that we really discover his nature.

The Covenant Restored (34:1-35)

Following the experience of the golden calf, perhaps involved in
Moses' new vision of God, God began the restoration of the broken
covenant. Only God could reinstitute the covenant. It had been his
gift originally. When it was restored, it could only be done by him.

The new experience (34:1-10).—In getting ready for the renewal
of the covenant, Moses was commanded to prepare two new tables
of stone. Moses was commanded to come up to God alone. The same
type of provisions were to have been made as were made earlier to
ensure that no one else drew too close to God.

In the experience of renewal, a major emphasis was made upon
the fact that God was "merciful and gracious, slow to anger, and
abounding in steadfast love and faithfulness" (v. 6). These characteristics were said to be worked out in his "forgiving" of sin as well as
in his justice. The full revelation of what this meant was not seen
until Jesus came. While iniquity might be visited upon the third and
fourth generations, his steadfast love reached out to thousands of generations. God's loving nature, even in the Old Testament, was seen
to be his fundamental nature. The statement that iniquity was visited
upon the third and fourth generations should not necessarily be understood as implying that children and grandchildren were to be punished
for the sins of their fathers. The people later understood it this way,
and Jeremiah and Ezekiel sought to counteract it (Jer. 31:29-30; Ezek.
18:1-4). The statement here in Exodus could be understood as referring to the nature of the world which God had made. The sins of

the fathers do show up in the practices of the children.

As a basis for the covenant renewal, Moses pled for a continued reassurance of God's presence and blessing through God's pardon. It is possible that we have here a repeated account of this need for the assurance of God's presence. Since much of this material was passed on orally for generations, it should not be considered surprising if major events were repeated in different circles lest there should be some lost. It may have been this which ensured their preservation. On the other hand, it is also possible that since the threat that God would not go with them had been so real, Moses was continually searching for a reassurance that God would be with them. It would have been a very human reaction.

God reassured Moses with the statement that the covenant was being reinstituted (v. 10). As a part of this covenant they were promised God's marvelous works as an evidence of his presence. These were not for the benefit of Israel so much as a witness to "all the people among whom you are." The power of God among his people is always a visible thing.

The appeal for purity (34:11-28).—These verses have offered a number of problems to interpreters. There is the implication that they were (or ought to have been) the same as the Ten Commandments in Exodus 20. They obviously are not, although there are many similarities. Further, there is some material here which appeared in the covenant code (20:21 to 23:19), but only a small amount of that code is reproduced here. This may be explained by a realization that part of these traditions may have been kept by some of the Hebrew tribes, while other traditions were preserved by others. Because of this, we need the entire collection of traditions to have the whole set of teachings. On the other hand, these particular laws have also been called the Ritual Decalogue, since the fundamental emphasis of these laws seems to have been upon ritual purity rather than righteousness. But this also seems to be an oversimplification.

Perhaps a more nearly correct solution can be found in a combination of these two approaches. It is quite likely that various traditions were preserved by various portions of the tribes of Israel and ultimately brought together under the inspiration and leadership of God. At the same time we need to recognize that in no way did they record or claim to have recorded everything that was said or done. A summary of these records would have served to remind them of the totality of God's messages and deeds. Thus, to limit what was restated to Moses in the renewal only to what was recorded here would be a mistake. To fully grasp what was said in the original covenant and in the renewal, we need to consider both sets of material.

The basic content of this material is dealt with in the commentary on 20:1-20 and 20:21 to 24:14. However, some additional ideas need to be considered here. The very fact of their covenant with Yahweh precluded their making a covenant with the people of Canaan. This applied to any kind of covenant, including the marriage covenant. In the ancient Near East, any covenant with another people involved their gods.

The commandment for the sabbath observance was also quite broad and very specific. They were to observe it "in plowing time and in harvest" (v. 21). These were especially significant for a society based upon agriculture. Their service of God was more important than their service of self. This is still a basic principle for anyone who seeks to serve God. God comes first.

The reflected radiance of God (34:29-35).—When Moses came down from the presence of God, he was unaware "that the skin of his face shone because he had been talking with God" (v. 29). This radiance was a symbol of the closeness of Moses to God. The attitude of the people toward him (v. 30) further reflected the awe with which they held him.

When Moses became aware of the awe on the part of his companions, he placed a veil over his face when he spoke with them. We are not told for how long this was necessary. Obviously, Moses did not have to continue the practice for too long. There is an interesting sidelight to this experience. Exodus seems to imply that Moses put the veil over his face so that he would not frighten his people with the radiance. Paul, on the other hand, says simply "Moses, who put a veil over his face so that the Israelites might not see the end of the fading splendor" (2 Cor. 3:13). Could it be that Moses for a time was trying to live on a past experience instead of on a continuing one? It is possible.

Thus it was that the experience of apostasy and rebellion came to an end. It came to an end by the action of God, not by the action of Israel. God renewed the covenant and through that experience Israel was restored to their relationship with him. But what happened was to become a pattern for Israel. They were to find over and over again how difficult it was to be obedient and faithful. It still is. But we have the advantage of the new covenant in Jesus. They had been redeemed from slavery. By God's grace, we have been forgiven and redeemed from sin.

Obedience That Delights the Spirit
35:1 to 40:38

The material in these final chapters, with only slight variations, duplicates that in Exodus 24:15 to 31:18. There are some minor variations of tense and person in verbs and pronouns, along with a few other differences which we shall note in the commentary material. The earlier chapters gave the commands for the worship equipment while these describe the actual construction. It is wise to study them together. The fact that the material is so similar has frequently caused students to skip this material altogether. This is regrettable, for some significant truths are found here.

Getting Ready to Begin (35:1 to 36:7)

In setting out to begin the work, Moses first set forth the sabbath commandment (35:1-3). The fact that this was the conclusion of the earlier section, while serving as the introduction here, was obviously deliberate. The last warning of the instructions was that the sabbath observance was the basic sign of Israel's covenant relation. The fact that Moses began with it here served to reaffirm that fact as well as to underscore that it was to be observed while they were actually involved in the construction project. There might have been a tendency to violate the sabbath on the grounds that they were involved in doing God's work. That was not a sufficient justification.

The prohibition against kindling fire on the sabbath is found nowhere else in the Old Testament. Since it is only used here, it may have been intended to prohibit the smelting or working with metals on the sabbath. This was a major task in the construction project, and there might have been those who would have sought to justify such activity. Doing God's work, even (or especially) highly skilled work, does not excuse us from obeying God. To the contrary, it makes it even more important that we obey him.

Next Moses issued a call for the basic materials needed for the task at hand (35:4-9). It is important to note that it was to be received only from those who were "of a generous heart" (v. 5). No one was to make an offering for this simply because it was commanded or even because it was needed. There is no way that slaves in Egypt could have had such valuable possessions. Obviously, these offerings were part of the treasure which they had asked for and received from the Egyptians.

In addition to supplies, there was also the need for workmen. This appeal was directed to "every able man among you" (v. 10) that they should give of their skills and time for the building project (35:10-19). Whatever a man's skill, there was something which he could do. God's kingdom still uses any ability which we might have. The call is still for "able" workers.

The response of the people was overwhelming (35:20 to 36:7). They came as the will and purpose led them, bringing their gifts to God. Again we see illustrated the paradox of human nature. These people who had so recently devoted their goods to the golden calf were now devoting themselves and their possessions to the service of God. The note that "both men and women" (v. 22) participated in this offering is especially significant. Since women usually played such a small part in the life of Israel, that they were mentioned here showed just how significant a part they must have played in this offering.

In response to the call for skillful workers, we first note Bezalel and Oholiab. Not only were they men of God-given skills; they had also been "inspired . . . to teach" (v. 34). Any work of God seems to require that some laborers must be used to teach and train others in using the skills God has given. We should also note that the workers came with willingness, with skill, and with intelligence (36:1-2). Without all three, the work would have suffered.

Of great significance is the fact that the offerings of the people became overwhelming. When it was reported that "the people bring much more than enough" (v. 5), steps had to be taken to end the offering. When God's people respond with joyous generosity to God's call for gifts, there should always be an overabundant supply.

Building the Worship Objects (36:8 to 38:31)

The reports of the construction of the tabernacle and the various objects of worship are given in detail in this section. At first glance it would appear that all of these things were done in sequence, one following the other. It is much more likely that the various tasks of sewing, building, and fashioning were all going on simultaneously.

Construction of such an elaborate tent in the wilderness would have been extremely difficult. It is possible that some of the later features of the tabernacle as it existed in Canaan, before the erection of the Temple, may have been read back into its initial construction. If this is true, the actual construction may have lasted over years rather than months. As we now have it, the record indicates a completely finished job carried out over a brief period.

The interior equipment was also made just as it had been described (37:1 to 38:20). The record of its construction has been set forth in logical sequence rather than in the order of the commands in the earlier section. The sequence of recording the construction begins with the ark in the most holy place, moves to the objects in the holy place, and finally out to the courtyard and its facilities.

One significant item added to this record is that the bronze laver was made "from the mirrors of the ministering women who ministered at the door of the tent of meeting" (38:8). In those times mirrors were made of polished metal. These had been given as their offering. The identity and function of these "ministering women" is unknown. The only other record of such is found in 1 Samuel 2:22, but that sheds no real light. In our ignorance all that we can say is that there was obviously some group of women dedicated to the service of God. What they actually did is lost to our knowledge. The statement that they "ministered at the door of the tent of meeting" is obviously anticipatory, for the tent of meeting had not been built until after they had made their offering. Whatever their function, it was obviously a service dedicated to God and one which continued after the erection of the tabernacle and on into the settlement in Canaan. If, as seems apparent, it came to an end after this, it was probably due to the fact that in Canaanite worship, women who served in their shrines were sacred prostitutes. Israel would certainly have done away with anything which might have given cause for such a misunderstanding.

The final accounting of the offerings and their use is of significance

(38:21-31). The first significance may lie in the fact that careful records were kept. God's business needs to be done in a businesslike way.

The treasures amounted to a little more than a ton of gold, almost four tons of silver, and almost three tons of bronze. Such a weight of metal would have been very difficult to transport on the number of wagons listed in Numbers 7:5-8, to say nothing of the tents, cloth, and wooden frames. It is highly possible that we are dealing here with weights before they had been standardized.

The Priestly Garments (39:1-31)

Three items of significance are recorded in the making of the priestly robes over and above the robes themselves. First, there is the recurring phrase "as the Lord had commanded Moses" (vv. 1,5, 7,21,26,29,31). It is hardly by accident that this was repeated seven times. This would probably have indicated to them the sacredness and the completeness of the making of the priestly vestments.

The second fact of significance is the statement that "gold leaf was hammered out and cut into threads" (v. 3) as a description of the technique used to manufacture the gold thread. Such a detail offers fascinating insights into the skills and handicrafts of the day.

The third detail of interest is the absence of any mention of the Urim and the Thummim (sacred lots) in the description of the breastpiece (see 39:8-21 and 28:15-30). This omission may be an indication that the sacred lots were natural stones and not shaped, fashioned, or otherwise manufactured. This becomes possible when we remember that the stones of the altar were to have been of such a nature (20:25). That which was left natural was considered to be more sacred than that which man had fashioned, since it was preserved in the form which God had given it.

Completing the Work of God (39:32 to 40:33)

When the work was completed, they brought all of the various items to Moses (39:32-43). This was apparently done to allow him to inspect them. The repetition of verses 42 and 43 lays particular force upon the fact that they had done the work exactly as they had been told. The listing of all the details stressed the fact of Israel's faithfulness and obedience to the minutest detail. The statement that "Moses blessed them" probably indicated that Moses was pleased with their obedience as well as with the quality of their work.

Following the completion of the work on the tabernacle, Moses was instructed to set it up (40:1-15). The divine command called not merely for the setting up of the tent but for its consecration.

The setting up of the tabernacle took place "in the first month in the second year, on the first day of the month" (40:17). This would indicate that it was erected eleven and one-half months after the actual exodus from Egypt (12:2,6). It would also indicate that the time spent at Sinai up to the setting up of the tabernacle was nine months (19:1).

The statement that "Moses erected the tabernacle" is probably not to be understood as his doing all of the labor. The weight would have made it well-nigh impossible for any one man to do such a task. It is more likely that the expression simply meant that he directed the job. It was at his authority that it was done.

The only detail added here is that of the washing of the hands and feet of the priests (40:30-32). The purpose was apparently to indicate that one's feet had to be clean before he could step into the holy place and that his hands must be clean before he could serve the Lord with the sacrifices. The outward cleansing probably signified that an inner cleansing was also necessary.

Perhaps one of the more sensitive statements in the entire episode of setting up the tabernacle is: "So Moses finished the work" (v. 33). Obviously, there had to be a real sense of accomplishment. But even more, in his initial call, Moses had been told that the only sign he would be given to prove that God was with him was that when he had brought Israel forth from Egypt, they would "serve God upon this mountain" (3:12). At last it had come to pass. The sign had been fulfilled.

The Ongoing Glory (40:34-38)

When the tabernacle was dedicated, the "cloud covered the tent of meeting." The symbol of God's presence had descended from the mountain and had moved to the tabernacle. This visible movement served to demonstrate to both Moses and Israel that God accepted and approved their labors. The glory of God so filled the tent that no longer could even Moses enter the most holy place.

Obviously, verses 36 through 38 were added at a later time by someone looking back at the long wilderness wanderings. They broke their camps and made their marches in obedience to the lifting or settling of the cloud. God, who had redeemed them and who had called them to himself, became their constant companion and guide.

The final reminder of the fire by night probably referred to the burning presence of God's glory.

In the beginning of Exodus, Israel was enslaved in Egypt and did not know that God was either near or aware of them. In the end of the book, they are free, redeemed people, on the way to the land of promise, accompanied and guided by the almighty God himself. So it has ever been. Those who have been redeemed by God are guided and sustained through the wilderness as they journey to the new land of promise. God always leads those whom he has redeemed.

Bibliography

General Works

Bright, John. *The Authority of the Old Testament.* Nashville: Abingdon Press, 1967. Reprint. Grand Rapids: Baker Book House, 1975.
————— *A History of Israel.* 2d ed. Philadelphia: The Westminster Press, 1972.
Francisco, Clyde T. *Introducing the Old Testament.* Rev. ed. Nashville: Broadman Press, 1977.
Grollengerg, L. H. *Atlas of the Bible.* New York: Thomas Nelson and Sons, 1956.
Ringren, Helmer. *Israelite Religion.* Philadelphia: Fortress Press, 1966.
Wright, G. E. *Biblical Archaelogy.* Philadelphia: The Westminster Press, 1957.

Commentaries

Cassuto, U. *Commentary on the Book of Exodus.* Jerusalem: The Magnes Press, 1967.
Childs, B. S. *The Book of Exodus.* Philadelphia: The Westminster Press, 1974. Old Testament Library Series.
Cole, R. Alan. *Exodus.* Downers Grove: Inter-Varsity Press, 1973.
Honeycutt, Roy L., Jr. "Exodus," *The Broadman Bible Commentary* 1 rev. Nashville: Broadman Press, 1969.
Plastaras, James. *The God of Exodus.* Milwaukee: The Bruce Publishing Company, 1966.
Rylaarsdam, J. Coert. "The Book of Exodus," *The Interpreter's Bible* 1. New York: Abingdon Press, 1952.